Praise for *Pain Rebel*

"Powerful. Raw. Practical. Dr. B once again challenges her readers to examine deeply personal and painful experiences in order to break free from complacency, embrace choice and thrive with intention. Like all of Dr. B's books, this book is easy to read, even if its subject -- pain, self-awareness, changing one's perspective and owning one's destiny -- is not. If you are looking to turn your pain into your power, *Pain Rebel* is for you!" ~ Melissa Jacob

"Dr. B has a keen sense of writing in a style that is simple and approachable, even when the message is heavy and otherwise difficult to deal with. As in her earlier books, *Pain Rebel* is a thoughtful and effective guide for moving beyond personal shackles and self-imposed limitations, to achieve growth, peace, and abundance." ~ Thompson Stimpel

"*Pain Rebel* extends to the reader abundant opportunity to create reflective, meaningful change in their life without judgment. Dr. B's words reflect honesty and respect while challenging the reader to rise up, assess and take action. I felt prompted to want to both do and be better after having read this book." ~ Christin Cofiell, LPC

"*Pain Rebel* is a great read for anyone who has gone through trauma in their lives; whether you are a timid teenager or a burned-out adult, everyone can learn from Dr. B." ~ Kat Wilbraham, Student

"This was such a motivating and inspiring read! Dr. B helps you transform from a Pain Collector to a Pain Rebel with the key takeaway (among many) that you will repeat what you don't resolve, and with a very teachable "aha moment" (again, among many) that pain is not the enemy and it is essential to help us heal. Thought-provoking and generating self-awareness, *Pain Rebel* is a must for anyone looking to break away from their old emotional contracts and take their POWER back." ~ Stacie Dumond

"*Pain Rebel* is a simple roadmap for life's most difficult journey; the quest to become the pickle I was always meant to be. Take this trip with Dr. B! You'll be glad you did." ~ Elizabeth Mansolillo

"*Pain Rebel* is an amazing book. The flow of different topics was so easy to follow. I myself will be using it on so many levels. I've let my circle of friends know about it so they can buy it for themselves. Congratulations on being a beacon of light for so many people, Dr. B. Don't ever stop!" ~ Salman Zafar

"Dr. B is a gifted author. Her writing is electric. I don't know how she makes every word hang and connect so well that I can't stop reading her books." ~ Loretta Stevens, Senior Executive Women's Network

"Us Pain Collectors, we tend to hold on tight and without realizing it. Dr. B took me on a journey to becoming a *Pain Rebel* in her authentic, engaging, and even fun step-by-step guide to freedom. Pain Collectors: Liberate yourselves and become a Pain Rebel!" ~ Lisa Middleton, MSW

"Dr. B talks about pain from a very personal place and invites her reader into an intimate conversation about where pain comes from, why every human must confront it, and how to manage pain in a transformative way. Whether you struggle with physical or emotional pain, *Pain Rebel* will give you concrete ways to reinvent your relationship with the past and the present so you can thrive in the future." ~ Heather Diemond Labbe

"All of us are Pain Collectors, carrying our guilt, shame, unworthiness and anxiety around like prized possessions. Torturing ourselves daily and endlessly. It's the human condition. My pain took me to the brink of madness. My tortuous path to recovery was a 25-year ordeal of drugs, psychedelic injections and ultimately shock treatments. Anyone reading **Pain Rebel** is luckier than me. Dr. B has written a guidebook showing us how to use our pain constructively, to elevate and not diminish our lives, to find joy in every moment and to become who we always hoped we could be. **All** of us need this book. Read it now and watch your life improve tomorrow." ~ Robert Phelan, CEO of TriPoint

"Like her other works, Dr. B's latest book, **Pain Rebel**, challenges you to look inside yourself and put her teachings into practice. Her down-to-earth writing style, personal stories, and in-book to-do exercises keep the pages and your highlighter flowing. You can't read it without one! ~ Darlene Williams

"Hell storms, suicide attempts, tragedies, manic work sessions, ostracizations and a horrific car accident to boot. And you thought you had issues? Dr. B survived (barely), learned (often the hard way) and changed (dramatically) to now live life to her fullest (yes, there are stories!). She shares her transformational processes here in **Pain Rebel** that have worked for so many; including herself. So, arm yourself for change, for the better, once and for all. There is pain and wishful thinking in all of us." ~ Thomas R. Fleury, Executive Management & Business Care, LLC

"I rebel therefore I am." ~ Albert Camus

Pain Rebel

How We Take Our POWER Back

DR. BRIDGET COOPER

ISBN: 978-0-578-71039-6

DEDICATION

∞

This book is dedicated to my inspirations for
following the path of a Pain Rebel:
My beautiful, badass daughters, Jessica and Elena.
May you always find the power of pain in
bringing abundant healing to yourself....and the world.

CONTENTS

Pain Rebel

TRIBUTES

> "Tell me, what is it you plan to do with your
> one wild and precious life?" ~ Mary Oliver

This book sprung from my own healing journey, so I feel compelled to begin by thanking those who invited me to sign pain contracts in the earliest moments of my life: My mom and dad. Now that I have softened my brittle and fragile self, I am grateful for the pain you levied on me. I have transformed it into something so deeply beautiful for the good of others. Without the damage I suffered at your hands, I may have never known how to share the gifts of empathy, conviction, and faith that brought me back from the brink. Though blind to it, you led me to true, powerful forgiveness so that I could teach it to others. Thank you.

To those who harmed me along the way, intentionally or haphazardly, thank you for reflecting back to me how damaged I was so that I might attend to my wounds. In wounding me, you reminded me to take time to heal my original pain.

To those who healed me along the way, intentionally or haphazardly, thank you for being an angel in my midst. We get through this messy, challenging world by slowing our step to help one another up when we've fallen.

To my Daughters: Unknowingly, you motivate me every day to be a better person than I was the day before, to heal my own pain so that I don't levy it on you. I cannot express in words how deeply I love and value you; instead, I hope to show you by guiding you to not be pain collectors and to live lives of joyful giving…and receiving.

To Lisa: Yeah, with every book I step more and more into the story that's been unfolding in me for years. What would I do without you to challenge, cajole, and heckle me? My often cantankerous but ever hopeful bff, get ready for that auspicious introduction that awaits. Maybe then I'll write that graphic novel about my crazy love life.

To Jim: I feel deep gratitude for whatever divine forces brought us together. I've learned more in our short time together than I thought possible and, in turn, have been reminded of love's power and grace. Thank you for pushing me to finish this, knowing how much healing that would provide, and for your ingenious ideas along the way. I love you three.

To Tania: I love how our paths crossed in pure serendipity and evolved into something I treasure. You somehow blend support with challenge, a trait that pushes me to be more aware and intentional in everything I do. Thank you for your unflappable commitment to me.

To Heather: I am so grateful for your incurably curious, reflective nature. Instead of writing in isolation, your questions, challenges, and reflections about life pushed me to dig deeper and offer more. I love being on this journey with you!

To Kim S.: There isn't anything you think I cannot do which 1) makes me laugh and 2) spurs me on to prove you right. Thank you for your friendship and support as I brought this book to life, a book that emanates from so many of our thoughtful walk conversations.

To Auntie Joanie: I am so grateful for your guidance, wisdom, and unwavering enthusiasm for my life and professional pursuits. You are truly my go-to person and I'm overwhelmingly grateful that I could start off as your shadow and end up simply as your biggest fan.

To Kelly G: You continue to be my faithful cover designer and creative influence. Thank you for translating my vision into reality, making the doorway to this material so inviting. You're the BEST!

To Paul Pita and the formerly Pita Group: Your concept for this book cover was brilliant! I thoroughly enjoyed brainstorming to take this from idea to product. It's now time to make YOUR book a reality and you can count on me to give my best right back to you.

To my Facebook Family: In this digital, virtual world, building authentic connections can prove fleeting and frustrating. I am blessed to bond with a collective of people near and far who understand my message and cheer me on at every turn. You guys ROCK!

To my Coaching Clients: Thank you for trusting me with your struggles, your worries, and your pain. In our work together, I watched as these techniques and perspectives transformed your lives. Not only did you create new contracts for a new life, you served as models so that others might follow in your footsteps. You're making the world a better place and I'm grateful for our shared path.

To my Editing Posse: You rock! Thank you for offering your tidbits and insights so that this book could be better because of you.

To You, the Reader: Thank you for taking a risk in buying and opening this book. If you follow the suggestions and exercises, I'm sending you a giant hug for trusting me with your healing journey. Life is too short, too precious, to live it in pain. I hope that this book gives you license to let that shit go. As you do, know that I am so grateful because the less pain we hold, the less we pass along. You are making the world a better place for everyone. Thank you.

How We Take Our POWER Back

Pain Rebel

PROLOGUE

About Rabelais' last words, "'I go to seek a great perhaps.'
That's why I'm going. So I don't have to wait until I die to start
seeking a great perhaps." ~ John Green, Looking for Alaska

The Universe has a way of putting you exactly where you need to be, whether you like it or not. I've long said that if you don't attend to the whisper in the ear or the tap on the shoulder, you'll get hit upside the head with a two-by-four. Over the past seven or eight years, I've had plenty of splinters in my head. I spent the first five years of that time writing one book right after the other. By the beginning of 2017, I'd penned five. In that same period, I'd suffered some devastating losses including the sudden deaths of my parents. I pressed on. I used my grief to fuel more activity. I possessed a frenetic energy that kept me treading just above the waterline.

I presented to large audiences all over the country, did television and radio shows, podcasts, and newspaper interviews. I even did a TEDx talk. I was on fire. I was living life large (in devotion to my tag line of the same words) and was looking forward to each subsequent adventure. I loved spending time with my teenage girls (shocking, right?) and had an abundance of friends I socialized with regularly. I was a mainstay at networking events and was an active volunteer in my heartfelt causes. I was **everywhere**.

And then I got hit by a truck.

No, really, I did. Okay, it's a little dramatic yet quite accurate.

Riding home from dinner with a friend, an Uber SUV plowed through a red-light into my door and flipped us on our roof. From the moment the car stopped, I suffered from nausea, dizziness, tinnitus, disorientation, confusion, and memory loss. The physical pain paled in comparison to the mental effects. I couldn't tolerate social situations. Forget networking; I couldn't even stand to be in a coffee shop at midday. My long, brisk walks became sluggish, miserable marches to the corner.

The Energizer Bunny™ became a sloth.

For months, I did everything the doctors suggested, everyone hoping my symptoms would pass. I found certain workarounds that made mandatory activities like mom-ing, driving, grocery shopping, and walking the dog tolerable: Chewing gum, limited computer time, avoiding reading, getting excessive amounts of rest, and a ridiculous array of alarms and calendars. Even my handwriting was affected. People used to compliment it and now it was barely legible and I habitually missed letters. I wasn't myself anymore.

Time passed sluggishly. First the three-month mark came and went; then it was the tell-tale six-month point when 90% of head injuries resolve.

Nothing.

The moment of truth came sometime after that: The neuropsychological test. It spanned three days of meetings because I couldn't tolerate the process for very long. Finally, she'd collected all the data she needed to document her findings. I felt so conflicted as I awaited the results. If she verified what I was experiencing, then I'd feel validated. But, if she did do that, then it would reveal the "invisible" damage.

Validation won.

I had a traumatic brain injury. My IQ dropped 25 points. No more Mensa eligibility for me. In processing the results, I learned all sorts of things about intelligence and understood why reading, writing, speaking, and paying attention were all troublesome to me. I maintained stellar verbal and analytical abilities, but my processing speed and retention were paltry.

More therapies were recommended and pursued. Nothing.

My light was dimmed. In this low-light, I went inward. I reckoned with my "new normal." How could I live in this world, contribute in the ways I'd dreamed, and be a good mom with my limitations? I had to adapt. Having written a book about the change process (*Stuck U.*), I returned to the basics. In order to adapt, I first had to do the hardest step of all: Accept. Accept life on its new terms. Accept that my brain wasn't what it was before. Accept that the things that were once effortless were now exhausting. Accept that I may always be like this.

Who was I if I wasn't engaging and spirited? Who was this new "mellow" person and what did she have to contribute to other people? How could I keep working? How could I keep my relationships strong and healthy? When friends and colleagues asked me how they could help, I simply responded, "don't forget about me." In my hiatus from my life, the loneliness was palpable.

Then COVID-19 wreaked havoc on our world. As I write this, we remain in isolation, socially distancing for the good of our communities. I haven't been hugged by another human being in almost two months…and I'm a hugger. So, what did I do? I hunkered down and decided to finish this book. Unlike my other manuscripts, this one has been sitting in note form for years. It was the project I planned to complete in the fall of 2018. Sadly, that truck hit me in late August 2018. My traumatic brain injury threw me off course and makes writing tortuous. Poetic that the book is about *pain*, huh? But I finally got to the point that however hard the writing was going to be, having an unfinished project was somehow worse. Luckily, acceptance had taken hold and I knew that waiting to complete it until I was "better" wasn't an option.

How We Take Our POWER Back

It's not lost on me that our COVID-19 experience and my journey with traumatic brain injury (like any chronic disease) are abundantly similar.

They both are contagious. We pass the virus…and pain…from person to person, often without even knowing it. In so doing, they each deliver their own brand of trauma. In the case of COVID-19, breath can bring death. We avoid others because they may cause us injury. In the months after the car accident, I was a wreck in the car, far worse when I was the passenger. I was afraid that every car was going to hit me. Both are invisible yet life changing. The car came out of nowhere, just like this pandemic. The disease itself can go undetected while still unleashing its deadly damage. We don't know when they will end, if ever. They've both delivered a new normal and we don't know how to change in response without rethinking every decision we make. Facing them each day is exhausting.

These are the ugly things.

We can't lose sight of the beautiful things.

They both force us inward…not just into our houses, but our hearts. For me, they've both provided heightened awareness about what trauma means, suffering, and discovering acceptance in a situation that I can hardly influence, let alone control. They've also both presented lessons in the indomitable strength and beauty of the human spirit. We've witnessed people helping people in unprecedented ways. Lord knows I didn't do this book draft alone. We've watched those with little share with those who have less. We've reconnected with family members through video calling and old-fashioned letters. We've returned to the basics of board games with family and walks in nature. We've faced our own mortality and been reminded to treasure the time we have and the gifts we have to give.

Pain Rebel is my gift to you. And my hope is that it's your gift to yourself.

Pain Rebel

What gift can YOU share with others?

The gift of compassion.

By "compassion" I don't mean "pity." I mean seeking to deeply understand the experience of another human being and then taking the necessary steps to ease their burden. To stand with them to help them fight the fight that may be at their door.

Just as this book was in its final editing phase, the world erupted in protest. Another black man in the United States was murdered by the people sworn to protect him…and it was caught on film for all the world to see. That man's name was George Floyd.

In witnessing his pain…and the pain felt by far too many for far too long…I got to thinking about *Pain Rebel*. What does this book have to offer in the context of our great upheaval as a nation and a world, staring down systemic racism as it tears at our peace and potential?

So fucking much.

Both are about easing suffering, taking decisive action, and for some, paradigm shifts…having hard conversations with ourselves and with others.

Pain Rebel teaches you how to work to disassemble your unconscious programming and destructive assumptions about pain so that you can be more aware, and therefore, more powerful. It's about changing frameworks and perceptions so you can see the raw truth and operate from it…and disassemble it because it's making life harder and limiting your true potential. We've taken for granted that how we see things is how they are; yet nothing could be further from the truth.

Pain Rebel is your wake-up call that you've been seeing pain through a prism that's flawed. With a new prism and better light, you can unpack…and transform…it. You can be part of a movement to relate to pain differently so that we can *all* live with less of it. This book doesn't stand in judgment or blame; it rests heavily on consideration and responsibility. Without understanding how we got here, we have scant chance of getting out. We need to be open to a new way of thinking about things, to find creative solutions to ingrained thinking and behaviors that no longer serve us, or our collective.

The same work is required of us to put an end to racial division and inequity. If we've been fortunate enough to not feel the sting of racism (or it's cousin, bigotry), we are compelled to now tune in. We have to look at the ugliness that's been right in front of us all along but we've (often unconsciously) chosen to ignore. This time, we get to do it better. We have guides who will show us the way out. To make lasting change, we have to change how we think about race and equality. We have to dig deep and elevate our awareness so that we can make conscious choice that serves us and our fellow humans.

Do we need to burn it all down and start over? I hope not. Just like I'll share in **Pain Rebel**, I believe that we can reckon with our mental models (whether they be about race/equality, or pain) and, with great care, challenge and excise the diseased pieces. From a place of seeing what was once unseen, we can vow to do better, be better. To operate from love, from understanding, and from peace. Love isn't passive and peace requires justice. Knowing this, we can rebel against the systems that lulled us into complacency because we see pain right in front of us and it demands healing and protection from more.

We are Pain Rebels and we won't stand for anything less than a revolution of thought…and practice.

"The Ego seeks to divide and separate.
Spirit seeks to unify and heal." ~ Pema Chödrön

1

ROAD AHEAD

"Do the best you can until you know better. Then when you know better, do better." ~ Maya Angelou

Liver and onions. Blech. Just typing those words made me want to retch in a bucket. You, too? In considering how to kick off this book, my mind wandered back to the time when my mother served this meal to me, rounded out by another smelly, unappetizing selection: smushy peas. I was six (I'm now 48) and I can still smell (and taste) the horror that confronted me on that round vessel that was to be my doom. I wasn't the most compliant child and, even then, I knew my own mind. I refused over and over again to eat any of it. My mom was resolute. She was raised by Depression Era parents; you ate what was on your plate. As I lifted that first forkful to my lips, I was certain that if I ate even a single morsel, it was coming back up *fast*.

And it did.

I'll spare you the gory details of what my plate looked like THEN, but you *know* it wasn't pretty.

Furious, my mom sent me to my room where I spent the duration of the night, the taste lingering in my mouth. I still recall being uncertain as to which was worse: the vomit or the food itself? Tough call, really, but I'm sure the mixture was one for the record books.

Why on Earth am I telling you this? Because I know that you might be thinking that reading a book about pain may be the equivalent of eating a plate full of liver, onions, and smushy peas.

Rest assured, it's not.

And not only because I'm confident that you'll enjoy my little excursions along the way that'll be like the buttered bread I wasn't offered to drown out the miserable meal, but because this book offers the way OUT.

Sure, I'll confront you with some truths that might be hard to hear, but then I'll walk you through how you'll shed the thoughts, patterns, and habits that are dragging you down. This book is going to lift you UP.

By the time you turn the last page, you'll never serve up or accept another nauseating offering, let alone attempt to stomach it.

Let's get started, shall we?

~ Is "Pain Rebel" for Me? ~

There are a billion books you could be reading right now, so how do you know that you picked up the *right* book? Easy. Let me ask you:

- Do you feel stuck in the same patterns, experiencing a lot of "déjà vu" moments?
- Do things bother you more than they "should?"
- Are you afraid of what the future has in store for you, at least partly because you predict that it'll be more of the same?

- Do you feel sensitive/reactive to slights by others?
- Do you ruminate on your past and your catalog of injuries and ways that life has been hard?
- Do you feel cheated by how life has turned out?
- Is your life a rollercoaster and you just want to get off?

If you answered "yes" (resounding or otherwise) to any of these questions, you're going to benefit in mind-blowing ways, feeling lighter and more powerful for having read this book. It's practical yet deep, and it'll require you to pause to soak it all in and apply its lessons to your life. You're worth it, trust me.

"You can't go back and change the beginning, but you can start where you are and change the ending." ~ C.S. Lewis

~ Big, Blue Samsonite Suitcase ~

Every year as a child, my grandparents flew me (sometimes my sister and me) from Massachusetts to spend a week with them in their posh, southern California home. Aside from my stuffed bunny, Paula, the one mainstay on each trip was a gigantic blue Samsonite rolling suitcase that I dragged through the airports, failing to dodge other passengers far too often. It's no exaggeration that I could have fit inside of it, so the scene was certainly entertaining to any onlooker. The only true benefit was that this was made of industrial-strength rigid material and no one (and I mean, NO ONE) had anything that looked like it, so baggage claim was a cinch!

That's what we look like as we make our way through life: Dragging our ridiculously-oversized baggage, bumping into each other with it, whether we mean to or not. But, unlike when we go on vacation for a week, we fail to unpack the things we shove inside. They stay there, crumpled up, getting heavier and smellier as time goes by. Cumbersome, they comprise our pain collections.

In the mid-1990s, I traveled to Russia to take part in a volunteer research trip. After a brief start in Moscow, we ventured off to stay with townspeople in a remote village about a day's train ride away. There was no running water or electricity in the homes, but there was plenty of one thing: Trauma. The elderly village residents recalled vividly the invasion by the Germans in World War II. Here we were, fifty years after the Armistice and you'd have thought that it was only a handful of months. Their grief was palpable, and deeply fathomable. They told harrowing tales of German soldiers ransacking their neighborhood, killing or capturing their men, and occupying their homes. Their eyes told the stories their words avoided. There was only one man in this village; he returned from the war injured, but luckily, alive. His face was a poignant reminder of the missing. There was *so much* missing. They felt their wounds like they were still being carved.

It's safe to say that we all have pain collections. Life has kicked us in the teeth more than once and these kicks often get buried. Sometimes we're just too "busy" to do the work required to let them go; other times they're too much to process so we conceal them just so we can survive. In our heads, we live in denial or straight up unconsciousness. We've all met people who pretend they don't have any pain; then it shocks us when it comes bursting out from the seams.

In our hearts, we are consumed with the fight impulse or, conversely, resign ourselves to defeat. We think facing the pain will be grueling, so we avoid it. Or we've been groomed to blame others. Blaming others feels comfy so why on earth would we do anything that would relieve that judgment? Maybe blame wasn't our game…perhaps it was shame instead? We internalized the blame, swallowing that bitter pill whole. If we do either of these enough, we earn the designation of

"Pain Collector." The hits just keep coming and our overwhelmed state seems permanent and inevitable.

~ Collecting It ~

Walking downtown one day, a friend of mine and I passed a row of quaint shops, most of which I'd never been in. Discussing this, she remarked that the restaurant midway down the was one she frequented when she was married. Then came the stories about what they'd eat and the memories they'd make after their family meal. Her voice trailed off as she looked wistfully into a past that was swept away by time…and the breakdown of the pitiful marriage she had been in. They'd married young and didn't have a clue as to how to have a healthy relationship. Instead of figuring it out, side-by-side, they blamed one another for everything, building resentments as far as the eye could see. Eventually, their marriage blew apart, dragging their children into its destruction. This once picture-perfect family was splintered and the members shared tense, sporadic communication, their love shrouded by their shared pain.

Recounting silently to myself about how she'd recently been doing the hard work of wrestling with her past in order to set it down, I looked again at my friend. Her jaw clenched and face tightened as the stone-cold truth hit her dead-on: If only she'd woken up earlier to how she'd been wallowing in resentment and hopelessness for so many years, she could have seen how she was creating her own misery before it swallowed her…and her family…up. Maybe she could have seen things differently and not gripped so tightly to her hurts, seeing as they just delivered more of the same. Instead, she collected them, stringing them together until you couldn't see where one ended and another began.

Many of us are Pain Collectors. We experience a pain or a set of pains…then we continue our journey, weighed down by that pain, only to find ourselves picking up new experiences of pain along the way. We create a laundry list of injuries, all the ways that the world (or a person) has worked against us, how we've been wronged, and the extent to which we now feel unworthy or incapable of happiness and peace. We often use our first heartbreak as a major touchstone, one that serves as our "why" for not taking risks or trusting others. This builds a narrative, the victim narrative. The filtration process only allows in more pain and sets us up to believe more deeply that this is just the way things are. Holding this as truth (even if the injuries are indisputable) saps us of our power to manifest another life for ourselves. It comes down to power: Do we want our pasts holding our own power from us?

Pain is inevitable. What we do with it is our choice.

In order to make good choices, we have to enhance awareness. This book digs into the awareness, builds it, and offers strategies and tactics to let go of a pain-dominated existence.

We all have moments we would never want replayed on the highlight reel of our lives; moments where we completely lost our shit and lashed out at other people, often those closest to us. Sometimes, we did so intentionally; other times, our wrath was unfortunate and wholly without intention.

In those moments when we likely harmed others, those "others" may have latched onto those unfortunate interactions and replayed them in the highlight reel of THEIR lives: retold those stories for their lovers, friends, therapists, and journals. That's how pain multiplies. It leaves us and goes to them, vice versa, and round and round and round we go.

Just as those regrettable moments of pain transfer don't define us, they ought not define others either. We can't go back, but we can move forward.

There are no do-overs…only do betters.

Releasing our emotional connection to those events gives us our power – and sanity – back. Yet, that's not what we've been taught.

Pain Rebel

We've been taught to *collect* it simply by being unaware of how it takes root in each of us and transfers from person to person.

~ My (Sob) Story ~

Sadly, I know a thing or two (or a million) about collecting pain.

Among those of us who have faced unthinkable trauma – at this point that's a significant portion of us – some are consumed by the fear it'll happen again. That, once again, we will be consumed by the fire of another. That we won't see what's coming toward us until it's too late. We get held in fear's stealthy grip, only to suffer over and over again by the movie playing in our heads of what is certain to come.

Is there another way?

I'm writing this book for a reason, aren't I?

The first time my mother saw my father beat me I was eight…Eight **weeks** old. He had been abusing my mother since early on in their torrid (her lens), tumultuous (his lens), toxic (my lens) relationship. Then I entered their sick dynamic, powerless to do anything to prevent my emotional and physical pain. When I was the ripe old age of one, the police came to our home and found me hiding in a closet, covered in my and my mother's blood. And then there were the sexual assaults: mine and my mother's. She found the resolve to leave him when I was two and a half but for her, love and pain were so intricately woven together that she never really broke free. As a result, I stayed joined to him, party to his psychological and sexual abuse until I reached adulthood and severed that tie.

My healing took decades longer.

How We Take Our POWER Back

I share this with you not to gain your sympathy, but your trust. Your trust that I know a thing or two (or a million) about pain and how it can manipulate our every thought, hijack our feelings, and invite some pretty ghastly behaviors. All this does not serve us or those around us except perhaps to be an example of what *not* to do. Heaven knows I did that *plenty*. The truth is that all of us, me included, have a long list of reasons that we could be complete asses. Quite a few of us habitually (and publicly) recount the items on that list, as though it serves us somehow.

Well, truth bomb: It doesn't.

In fact, what it does is it sucks the air out of the room and the joy right out of our too-short lives. Worse yet, they win. Who's "they?" All the "theys" who have kicked, disregarded, maligned, and otherwise injured us along the way. They WIN. How? By continuing to hurt us, sometimes long after they've left this planet. Still, there we stand (or cower), trying to hold them accountable for all the crap they foisted upon us.

I know first-hand how draining and downright self-defeating this well-intentioned behavior can be because I honed it into an art myself. And I watched those around me literally kill themselves by drowning in this re-visitation process.

Before it could finish me, I finished it with it. I coaxed that proverbial horse back into its barn and reclaimed my life, my *power*. How? Well, if I covered that now it would spoil the rest of the book! Hang tight and get ready to see the path unfold to your healing journey to your membership in the "Pain Rebel" Club. Membership ain't free, but neither is being a pin cushion for all the things and people who have injured you. The move from Pain Collector to Pain Rebel is a mighty shift, but a wholly worthwhile one.

"Where there is no struggle, there is no strength." ~ Oprah Winfrey

Pain Rebel

~ What to Expect ~

It's pretty simple, really. This book sets out to get you from where you *are* to where you *want to be*, even if you hadn't yet defined exactly what that looks like. Lucky for you, I've reduced some of the heavy lifting and defined it for you. You're reading this because, down deep, you want to go from being a collector of pain to someone who defines your own relationship to it. It answers the following:

What do we do in regard to pain versus what we **can** do?

How we got here, why we stayed here, and how can we get out?!

Know this: It doesn't matter if your pain was the result of the actions of others…or your own. It doesn't matter if you have pain that's a month old…or you've been holding onto it for a lifetime. This book is your ticket OUT.

To get you out, I'm going to break things down into chewable chunks. First, I have to present you with the symptoms of our broken relationship to pain, so you'll be convinced we do, in fact, have a problem that needs solving. Second, I'll define the issue itself. Then, I'll spend the rest of the book teaching you how to embody the traits of a Pain Rebel.

~ Roadmap ~

I'm nothing if not a *practical* rebel. I require a plan, a map. I'll take a leap and guess that you're a smidgen like me and might benefit from one, too. So, buckle up, Buttercup: Here it comes.

You're welcome.

How We Take Our POWER Back

In my third book, **Stuck U.**, I presented my client-tested, 5-step model for change. The five steps are: Awareness, Acceptance, Analysis, Action, and Adjustment.

First, you notice there's something wrong (Awareness).

Second, you reconcile your situation. You take full responsibility for the decision to change as well as how you got here in the first place, knowing that if you got here, you could get out (Acceptance).

Third, you take stock of where you are, where you want to go, your resources and encumbrances, and lay out a plan for moving forward (Analysis).

Fourth (you're almost there, but here's the doozy!), you take steps to change yourself, your situation, your life (Action).

Fifth and finally, you assess your progress and make any refinements to the changes you've made so you can live the life you want (Adjustment).

Scared? Overwhelmed? *Breathe.* This process is doable and desirable over your current situation or you wouldn't have gotten this far in the book.

Being a Pain Rebel means tackling these five steps in order to transform our relationship to pain, taking back our power and promise in the process. How do you move from being a Pain Collector to a Pain Rebel? What does that bridge look like?

Following this change model, you'll use the rest of this book as your roadmap and constant companion, answering two pivotal questions:

~ What has to shift conceptually for you to transform your relationship to pain from Collector to Rebel?

Pain Rebel

~ What are the steps to get from here to there?

It's kismet, really, that I was named Bridget. When I meet people (or I'm on the phone with customer service reps), I'm invariably asked how to spell my name. My response? Cross a bridge. Get it? Put a cross (t) after a bridge. Sounds like "Bridge-it."

I know, I know, *brilliant*. Thanks, Mom and Dad!

It's also what I'm all about: Crossing bridges. Joining the space between "here" and "there." Finding a way. Bringing people to their destinations. Providing a view of where you've been and where you're headed.

Imagine a beautiful expanse of land just across the way. A green, lush field, bursting with color and life. You want to escape the stinky, muddy swamp you're rooted in and move yourself onto that divine landscape at the edge of your view. That's when you see it! A white, arched bridge with supportive railings on either side that leads from your swamp to the gorgeous expanse. How slowly you pause, reflect, gather strength, gaze ahead and behind is all entirely up to you.

This book provides the bridge itself.

How you traverse it is completely under your control.

I know you've been hoping for a better existence. Your hopes have been dashed, day after day, hurt after hurt.

My hope is that you'll place your hope where it belongs: In the divinely placed power of your own feet to move you out of darkness into light.

In this case, the darkness I speak of is a broken relationship with pain; the light is the mending of it, freedom from its oppression, dominance, and blinding nature. It's the land of living a more abundant, joyful, peaceful, FREE life.

How will you walk that expanse? One deliberate step at a time. With a splash of help from yours truly, you'll:

~ **View pain differently.**

~ **Raise your consciousness about your connection to, and collection of, pain. When you are conscious, you have power...the power to choose...and to change.**

~ **Embody the art of letting go.**

What do I want for you? I want you to commit to a relentless, passionate pursuit of something different and better.

~ Unless ~

Unless you're not ready. It's possible that it's warm under the blanket of your own suffering and disappointment and the idea of venturing out might be too much right now. You've gotten used to defining life, yourself, and the people around you in a certain way. You've got a story that makes sense. You're not looking to get swept into some new way of seeing things. You're hurting but it's comfortable somehow.

It's okay. You don't have to do it now. Tuck this book up on a shelf, somewhere you'll see it every now and then. When life is dragging you into the dim, know that the answers await you when you're done with this script and you wish to write another for the remaining scenes of your epic story.

"Do not worry that your life is turning upside down.
How do you know that the side that you are used to
is better than the one to come?" ~ *Rumi*

2

THERE'S SOMETHING GOING ON

"There comes a point where we need to stop just pulling people out of the river. We need to go upstream and find out why they're falling in." ~ Desmond Tutu

We are in pain. As a culture, in our communities, in our homes, and as individuals.

When we show up at the hospital with a persistent high fever, our doctor knows we are fighting a physical infection. Given the startling statistics I'm about to share, it's clear we are battling an emotional, spiritual, and social infection. Tragically and collectively, we're losing.

I suppose it's pointless to expend energy convincing you that pain is a problem since you're reading this book. And maybe I'm making a crazy leap here, but I'm venturing to say that you, my dear reader, are in some degree of pain that you'd rather not be.

You've got a lifetime behind you of defining yourself, people around you, the world, and every experience in a certain way. Those definitions spur patterns of thought, feeling, and behavior. What you think about things basically IS the world you experience. Sometimes these patterns have served you, sometimes not so much. Sometimes "not so much" careened you into a steaming shit storm of heartbreak, disappointment, dysfunction, and downright failures.

How do I know? I've witnessed a whole mess of disheartening and downright destructive patterns with my clients...and myself.

What's at the root of these patterns?

~ Our Discomfort with Discomfort ~

We are uncomfortable with being uncomfortable. Why? Because our culture sanitizes life so we equate "messy" with "tragic." The truth is, messy IS life…. because life IS messy.

We've been brainwashed to view discomfort as being bad, so we do anything to remove it. The medical community reinforces our broken relationship to pain. They medicate it or deny its existence. They can't tolerate or witness suffering. They need to make things comfortable.

When I suffered a traumatic brain injury, I saw a series of doctors. They tried all the usual strategies and they all proved ineffective at fixing my symptoms. To say I was frustrated is the understatement of the year. When I expressed my frustration (through tears, mostly), more than one provider suggested that I go on anti-depressants.

Um, what?

My frustration turned to exasperation. Why was the solution to my symptoms (nausea, dizziness, visual disturbances, tinnitus) a mood-elevating drug? Well, it wasn't. That drug wasn't going to *fix* what I was experiencing; it was simply going to *quiet* me so that I didn't express the sadness I rightfully felt about having a debilitating head injury. I was going to make things more comfortable for *them*, for sure. For me? Not very likely.

Now, I'm not knocking anti-depressants. When used properly, they can literally save lives. My irritation lies in our discomfort with seeing logical emotion in response to a hurtful situation. We want to quiet it, fix it, so we numb it in whatever way we can.

We have it all wrong: Discomfort is good and useful. Discomfort heightens our awareness of problems. It tells us that action is required, that we need to adjust something we are thinking or doing that is hurting us. Discomfort is temporary. It's like a fever: it's a signal not a disease. Discomfort isn't the problem. What we choose to do with it unleashes our potential for greatness…and joy.

What if we saw pain as positively as we do pleasure? What if the next time a friend confided in you that they were experiencing pain and you said, "That's awesome! What are you going to do with it?"

Yeah, okay, they might **un**friend you.

Truth is, that's the very sentiment that will empower them to be in a better place after the pain than they were before it. What if you reassured them that they were more than capable of tackling the challenge in front of them? That running from the pain is another way of saying that we don't believe that we are capable of handling it.

In this chapter, I'm tackling the destructive ways that pain shows up, gets mishandled, and destroys us, individually and as a collective. The destruction materializes when we internalize or externalize it without unraveling and addressing it on our own.

You see, we are capable. We are meant for adversity. We are better for change.

How We Take Our POWER Back

Take pickles, for instance. Pickles start off as healthy, green, delectable cucumbers. There's not a thing wrong with cucumbers, of course. They are regarded members of the vegetable family and hold their unique place in the food universe. In salads, veggie platters, and how my mom got me to eat them: As peanut butter boats. Maybe you like them, maybe you prefer pickles or the other way around. We can agree on one thing: Pickles and cucumbers are quite different. Why? The brine.

In order for cucumbers to transform, they require brine. To elevate their way into specialty burgers and Cuban sandwiches and in the hands of pregnant women the world over, they need to sit and allow the brine to do its magic.

If you're sitting in brine of your own right now, fear not: Maybe you're just a pre-pubescent pickle.

Soak. Emerge. Be the victorious pickle you were meant to be.

~ Self Destruction ~

A guy I used to date teased me endlessly about how I always tried to "shove ten pounds of shit into a five-pound bag." I saw this as overachieving and an enviable level of productivity. He saw how crazy it made me when there just weren't sufficient hours in the day to get it all done and to my high standards.

What I hadn't faced was that this behavior was rooted in pain. I was running on the hamster wheel of life trying to stay busy so I wouldn't find myself feeling too much of anything. I was convinced that feeling things deeply would be my undoing. So, I kept busy doing and doing and doing.

We deal with pain in pretty predictable ways. If we thrust it upon the world, it comes out as anger, stress, and violence. If we keep it inside it shows up as suffering, denial, procrastination, and isolation. Let's root out the mess on our insides first, shall we?

~ Suffering ~

Returning to our pickle example, suffering is a different matter altogether because it's not at all about transformation.

When our core wounds are big enough, they resemble a crater. We stuff the crater with stuff (accomplishments, relationships, money, good looks), but it never fills. Left alone at this depth, we create a narrative of suffering.

We fail to realize that the only solution is to reduce the size of the crater in the first place.

If not, we set ourselves up for more and more suffering. How does that work? We wire our brains to see that suffering means reward; the more we are enduring, the more that we will acquire in the form of attention, compassion, pity, or accomplishments and objects. The more we hurt, the more we benefit. It's a fucked-up Pavlov's dogs' experiment. One psychologist named people who do this, "injustice collectors. They are prone to perceive insults and failures as cumulative, and often blame them on one person or one group" (Meloy, NY Times, 2017). Collecting these injustices is a subconscious choice. Now, don't start wallowing in shame if this sounds uncomfortably familiar. There's no sense in losing yourself in self-recrimination for things you did when you were asleep. You were *asleep*. With some help from the book, you're waking up. That's precisely why we're here…to create awareness so you can make a different choice. To make an informed choice, we must know that:

What we allow we must endure.

How We Take Our POWER Back

When we hold onto the pain of the past and foresee a future plagued by it, we resign ourselves to a life of suffering. In the darkness with our eyes tightly shut, we fail to see the light at the end of the tunnel.

Suffering is the equivalent of the cucumber bathing in a substance that, instead of transforming it into a pickle, just disintegrated it into a pile of mush. When we believe that suffering is what we were destined for, we adopt a narrative of suffering.

Straightforward yet pervasive, this pain collection pattern plagues us. Simply put, those stuck in its clutches believe that life is pain, that they are the victim in their own life story. No matter what they do, they will always, yet again, find themselves on the raw end of every deal. Please don't confuse this with pessimism; they share some basic features (believing that bad things are likely coming) but they part ways in the gravitational pull of the suffering narrative: The individual whose life is dictated by the storyline has no volition to change anything. They are powerless. Suffering is inevitable, and sometimes even deserved. They are being punished for named and unnamed sins, transgressions, faults.

We use other people's behavior to justify our own. They did such and such so we "must" do this and that. We position our response on a "warranted" platform. *Their* behavior warrants *our* behavior. Take, for example, someone who cuts us off in traffic.

We tell ourselves that ***of course*** we feel a certain way so we ***must*** respond in kind. Calling them names, honking our horn, or cutting *them* off when we get the chance, all meet the ***of course*** and ***must*** threshold. We seek confirmation of our thinking by telling others, and being the agreeable people they are, they tell us we are right to have done what we did.

Our inner voice scratches at the door, though, revealing the empowering truth that simply because it's ***justified*** doesn't mean it's *required*. We *do* have choice…so there IS another way. We don't have to succumb to suffering to prove how right we are.

Take my ex-husband, for instance.

We had what they called a "high-conflict divorce." My ex-husband was (is) convinced that I was (am) the devil personified and was so openly hostile about this opinion that it was deeply wounding our children. It got to the point that a court-appointed official was assigned to our family to help us navigate the conflict in a manner less injurious to our kids. This official and I had a number of deep conversations that kept pointing back to the same target: Was my ex-husband capable of changing his behavior and under what conditions?

My answer was decidedly "no."

Please know that I believe that people *are* capable of profound change…if they **want** it. In his case, in order to *want* to change, he would have had to have reached the conclusion that his behavior had some part in the misery he was experiencing. Because why change *your* behavior if you're not part of the problem? To reach that point, he'd have to let go of the deep-seated notion that I was the source of all bad things in his world. Once he softened on that, and simultaneously admitted his part in things, he'd then be forced to face the sorrow he inflicted on those he claimed to love. Oh. My. God. That, my friends, is not for the faint of heart.

What's far easier? Staying put in the suffering we've come to know so well.

~ What's That River in Egypt? ~

People steeped in suffering have one strange bedfellow: denial. What do we deny? Our agency, our ability to change our circumstances. We hide from the pains we've collected and that the nagging voice in our head that doubts our capacity for greatness. I call these foes our "monsters." Much like the monsters under the bed (or in our closet) growing up, we are terrified of that which we imagine but cannot see. If we can find it within ourselves to confront the truth that we have more power than we give ourselves credit for, what do we do next?

You start chasing your monsters.

You do *what?*

You chase your damn monsters. Monsters don't own the chase game. They grow in your fear. They can only be used to hurt you if you are afraid of or in denial of whatever they are holding. Running from something, by definition, keeps us connected to it by referencing our progress by its location.

When you face your monsters, you move into a state of allowing discomfort in the range of ways it shows up: as fear, anxiety, sadness, and anger. It's counterintuitive, really, that in doing this, you take away their power over you. You grow in courage and love for a better, brighter day. That growth is authentic, brave, and beautiful.

Life stinks sometimes. Our job is to face it. To work through it. To reach out to the resources around us. We can't hide from life. That doesn't make the pain less or easier, it actually makes it worse. In trying to avoid it, we compound it. Facing, dealing with whatever we feel **when** we feel it, that's what makes us warriors. If we trade the slow burn for the swift agony we fear, we realize that we are stronger than we thought.

~ Numbness ~

Too often, we get stuck fearing the swift agony, thinking it will consume and drown us. So, we shut out the world and all the people and things in it that might hurt us. We want more than anything to feel safe. Unfortunately, shutting out the world also means shutting down our emotional response system. The problem? Numbness, despite our imaginings to the contrary, is not a solution to pain.

Pretending that everything is hunky dory when nothing could be further from the truth forces you to shut down, denying your own experience, at least in the face of others. The absence of feeling – or numbness – is another form of pain. Why? Because human beings are sustained by love and connection. Numbness serves as a barrier to connection, to love, and therefore is against our human nature. Resisting who we are creates discomfort (pain). We hold the dull ache, even though the swift agony we fear comes at a far lesser cost.

The longer it takes you TO sit in the pain, the longer you'll sit IN it. As a society, the U.S. is plugged in but checked out. We break away from the tough stuff life hands to us through distraction. We talk all day long about our golf game or a post on social media but resist the deeper, more meaningful exchanges. Afraid of sharing our inner experience with others who might reject us, by a world that might not give us what we deserve.

Hiding from pain is just another way we bring more of it to ourselves simply by missing out on the fullness of life, delaying the inevitable. Speaking of postponement…

~ Procrastination Nation ~

As I write this section, I'm struck by its timing in my own life. What's that saying? Art imitates life? Yup. Well, if you can call this book "art" then it fits my situation and this heading perfectly.

I started crafting this book years ago, passionate about its message of healing and power. Along the way, abundant distractions emerged: Work with clients, a TEDx talk, children, house projects, LIFE. Care to hear the messy truth? No greater impediment presented itself than yours truly. Me. The incessant flurry of thoughts and emotions around this tender topic. *My* pain. *My* struggles. MY perpetual rebellion from the tendrils of the pain legacy encoded in my DNA. The three-ring circus of self-defeating distractions that derail us all at one time or another is my most unwelcome companion. Oh, and a traumatic brain injury caused by an automobile accident that causes dizziness, nausea, headaches, and visual disturbances…all things that get a little in the way of focusing and writing.

Simply put, I've been procrastinating *writing about* pain *because of* pain. Deep, right? And deeply true. I'm an annoyingly passionate proponent of facing down your demons so I'm putting my money where my mouth is so here I sit, typing away. The symptom of procrastination will NOT win.

How about you? Where is pain stopping you?

If you're like a lot of my clients, it impedes you in several areas. Maybe you have a project (book, educational program, fitness goal) that you talk about but never actually set into motion. You say how great life will be when you get around to getting around to that. In my coaching circle, we call these items "tolerations." Tolerations are those nagging projects or things that you've neglected to take action on that are weighing you down. You're tolerating them hanging there and, in the process, you're internalizing messages about your own incompetence or unworthiness.

Speaking of internalizing messages, I have to tell you about my guest bathroom.

First off, I love painting. Not just a little love…it's an obsessive love. I get such satisfaction from painting because of how it transforms a space from blah to beautiful in a matter of hours.

I've painted my guest bathroom three times in 13 years, each time prettier than the last. What does this have to do with procrastination? Well, let me tell you about the baseboard trim. I painted that, too, but during the second paint job, it separated from the wall and I couldn't get it nailed back in place. So, what did I do? I pushed it into place and *leaned* it up against the wall, exposing an annoying gap that attracted dust and dog hair like a moth to a flame. No matter what clean up and decorating I did, the room never looked finished or tidy because of the half-assed trim job.

I'm embarrassed to say that it took SEVEN YEARS (yes, I said, seven YEARS) of looking at this abomination of a "little detail" DAILY for me to make that phone call. Guess how long it took him to set it straight and make my bathroom look the oasis I'd envisioned? Seven MINUTES. Minutes. WTF, Bridget?

Sound familiar?

Maybe you envision having a meaningful relationship at some point in the future, after the kids are grown or your heart heals, or you lose that weight…or…or. Regardless of the infinite reasons you have for putting off till tomorrow all the things that will bring you the thing you say you want, you're what I call "maybe someday-ing" yourself. And that, my friend, is a symptom of unresolved, unhealed, and often unexamined pain holding you back from risking more of the same.

~ Hooked on Connection ~

Our relationships may be what we complain about most, but they are also the strongest predictor of our health and longevity. Harvard's Grant & Glueck famous 80-year longitudinal study on adult development had two main findings:

1) Relationships equate to happiness.

2) Alcoholism is the root of all evil.

It's been said that addiction comes from loneliness, feeling disconnected from others. Loneliness isn't being alone, of course. You can be alone and feel quite connected. And you can be with others and feel dreadfully lonely. For those prone to addiction, loneliness is perilous. If you've been raised to struggle with (or felt unworthy of) meaningful connection, substances (and other addictions) become your faithful companion, your jagged solace. When the world walks out, Jack Daniels walks in. Or Budweiser. Or Absolut.

Just ask my boyfriend.

To meet him, you'd never think he suffered from a profound sense of loneliness. He can't go anywhere without running into people who warmly greet him and treat him with great regard. Every stranger is just a friend he hasn't met. He draws his enviable warmth from the sunshine-y aspects of life.

But loneliness occupies his shadows.

Like many who wrestle with addiction, if you peel back the layers of his effusive charm, you see an injured soul that has felt alone, rejected by those he sought comfort and love from. In that rejection, beautifully tender people like him reach for a substance to numb the pain, to accompany them in the darkness. Their "friend" then consumes them with every swallow.

Early on, I named his addiction, that "friend" whose personality takes over when he's drinking, "Chuck." [To all those out there with that name, I apologize for what I'm about to say.] Chuck rhymes with "fuck," of course, and I couldn't stop muttering that particular word when I found out quite suddenly that the man I fell in love with was consumed by this darkness. This particular naming convention came in quite handy in distinguishing between my boyfriend and this stranger I felt incredible disdain for. It allowed us to talk about Chuck without disparaging my boyfriend.

And, oh how I disparaged (…and whales are "big") Chuck.

Like many of those in a relationship with an addict, I felt saddened that the connection, the love, I offered wasn't enough to soothe his pain. That I wasn't enough to heal his hurts. That he chose his liquid mistress over me.

But that's not the choice he was making. That was my outdated programming rising to the surface. Programming earned through a lifetime of being in codependent roles that said it was my job to save others, and that if I was worthy, those around me wouldn't be in pain.

The truth was that his addiction long preceded me and far overpowered me. Given that I was writing this book when we met, I knew plenty about the insane "not enough" thinking I was entertaining. I understand where pain comes from, how it takes hold, and how it gets released. His addiction wasn't mine to heal; and alcohol wasn't the problem, either.

His **pain** was.

And until he faced it, it was going to keep running…and ruining…his life.

And he's not alone in this painful journey. Like in his case, addiction takes hold early on. Just take a look at these alarming statistics:

- Rates of illicit drug use are highest among 18 to 25-year olds.
- 90% of adults with an addiction began before age 18.
- As of 2011, 20.6 million over the age of 12 had an addiction (not including tobacco); 6.8 million have a mental illness.
- Alcoholism is down, but illicit drug use is up. Specifically, marijuana, prescription drug, heroin, and methamphetamine use are up; cocaine use is down.

How We Take Our POWER Back

It doesn't end when these young people grow into adulthood. And it's not an inner city or minority issue as has been a common misconception. According to the CDC, cirrhosis, opioid use and addiction, and suicide are epidemics among the white working class.

An addiction of sorts that affects the majority of Americans is that to food and unhealthy eating habits. According to the Centers for Disease Control (CDC), over 70% of Americans are overweight, while over 40% are morbidly obese. Stanford Health care reports that 300,000 deaths per year in the United States can be attributed to obesity. Obesity and depression are linked: 43% of those with depression are obese (CDC).

The CDC reported in 2020 that suicide rates have risen for thirteen years in a row. There are on average 123 suicides per day in the United States, 22 of them are former or current members of our armed services. Ninety people per day die from opioid overdoses (sources: U.S. Bureau of Justice Statistics, National Sexual Violence Resource Center). In recent years, middle-aged Caucasian Americans have seen the highest increase in "deaths of despair" (suicide and drug overdoses).

What causes deaths of despair?

Experts think it's our stressful society combined with the easy fixes to those feelings offered by the medical community that underlies deaths of despair (Dr. Anne Case, Princeton). Our brains change in response to stress, making us more emotional, less empathetic, and more prone to habit development, including addiction. Consequently, we find it harder to handle stress, and the circle goes round and round.

Managing our emotions at work, at home, and in our communities is critical to our health...and our *safety*. But, how equipped are we to do that?

As children, many of us were told not to display our emotions, especially boys. It's no wonder boys become violent as men. It's become a natural response to emotion because they weren't taught how to adequately deal with uncomfortable emotions, or if they were, it was through the anger channel. Hate is far easier to express than love when we're in pain. Women, on the other hand, receive the prevailing message that we need to soothe others by ignoring our frustrations.

Or, contrarily, we indulge them to prove our discomfort…and we become drama seekers. You know what that looks like. Every tiny frustration becomes a national emergency, creating incredible chaos and disruption. Every phone call or text kicks off with, "can you believe what so and so did/said/didn't do/didn't say…..?!" Intense doesn't even begin to describe these exhausting exchanges.

~ Volcanic Eruptions ~

Whoops! I'm getting ahead of myself by addressing what it looks like when we externalize our hurts. Pain externalized expresses itself as anger, stress, and violence. As integrated as they are, let's tackle them one at a time…

~ Stop the Madness ~

Emotions serve to inform us about what's going on behind the scenes. There are no wrong emotions. Misplaced? Perhaps. Disproportionate? Sometimes. Overused? Absolutely. Anger is one of the most popular out-of-whack feelings, cropping up to protect us from anything or anyone getting close enough to injure us. When we feel threatened, frightened, or injured, we tend to lash out. In turn, we might show up as mad at the world (and every last soul in it) or just zero-in on a select few. Our madness might come out as cruelty toward those we feel are "deserving," or then again, we could spread it like wildfire, catching anything in its path.

How We Take Our POWER Back

When we are in anger-mode, we are wearing our pain on the outside for everyone to see, often injuring others as we lash out, and shut out. People who want to get close to us can't, and that hurts, them and us. When anger is our go-to emotion to deal with our pain, when we deny the range of more vulnerable emotions that might crop up, we can fool ourselves into thinking that we are protecting ourselves. In fact, we are adding to our pain by shutting out the very actors that could heal us: Ourselves and other people.

How has it come to this? The hard reality is that the people closest to us are also the people most apt to cause us harm.

~ Intimacy Wars ~

We are all born from connection, healthy or toxic. If our connections are healthy, we have a fighting chance for happiness and peace in this world; if not, we have to fight for it.

I fought for mine.

Born and raised in a violent household, I ran into the arms of similar intimate partner relationships in my adulthood. And, unfortunately, I've been a bystander, confidante, and support system for a number of people caught in this dangerous, debilitating web.

It is in our relationships that we discover the crux of our emotional and physical health. The happiness we enjoy in our relationships has an instrumental influence on our health.

Pain is evident not just in the bodies and minds of those being abused following the abuse itself, but in the abuser and sometimes in the perpetuation of the dynamic itself. Reactivity, hair-trigger tempers, infidelity, bailing on relationships before they've even had a chance: Every last one of these symptoms destructively mask pain. We hide from – and in – relationships to mask – or indulge – our pain. We are the walking wounded and this wreaks havoc on our most intimate of endeavors.

Our job in a relationship (of any kind) is to awaken one another to our stored pain so that we can shed it. NOT add to it. NOT deepen it. NOT validate our worthiness for pain, suffering, and a pervasively painful existence. That's all myth and misunderstanding.

Rather, relationships exist to direct us to where it still hurts so we can lighten our load. We shouldn't look to *avoid* people who awaken that in us because that means that our hurts will continue to lay dormant, waiting to be triggered. If I am made sad by people who reject me and, in response, I only link up with people who are certain to never do so, I never heal that injury…I just cover it up. I never actually feel *WORTHY*, just *SAFE*. No, safe isn't a bad thing. Our focus on it is just a symptom of our Pain Collector status.

Speaking of Pain Collectors, I must introduce you to my parents.

My mom and dad entered their relationship injured, broken, needy, and without any sense of themselves except in relationship with a lover. They saw themselves as extensions of one another, carving their identity through the other's perception of them. They brought considerable pain into the relationship, experienced, and then doled out plenty within it. My father beat my mother early on in their relationship, then I was drawn into their toxic web. Although the marriage ended, the connection between them never did. Their pain pact lived till my mother breathed her last breath.

Effects of childhood trauma pervade far into adulthood, particularly when there were multiple events (Copeland et al., JAMA Network Open, 2018). Further, those exposed to trauma "have a higher chance of repeated trauma exposure and potential perpetration" (Gelkopf, JAMA Network Open, 2018). What are these effects of childhood trauma? Anxiety, depression, and all of the crutches we grab onto to dull the pain. The more we suffer as children, the bigger the cumulative damage. Instead of building healthy thinking and coping mechanisms, young victims of abuse, neglect, and trauma form maladaptive scaffolding (Adverse Childhood Experiences [ACE]). Chronic physical and mental illness, relationship disruption, and substance abuse are common complaints of those with high scores on the ACE inventory. Feelings of hopelessness and helplessness tattoo the souls of trauma survivors. Before we can redesign the tattoo, we have to examine its design.

And that design is anchored in our relationship to fear.

~ Anxiety & Stress ~

Anxiety is based in fear, fear of the things we cannot control. The World Health Organization (WHO) says that anxiety is the most common mental illness on the planet. What does anxiety produce? Stress. What does stress produce? Anxiety.

Simply put, stress (and therefore, anxiety) is all about control.

Stress is the pressure felt when what you *want to* control is greater than what you *can actually* control.

Studies have shown that cardiovascular disease is linked to having little perceived control as compared to the number and level of demands placed upon people. When there is more on your "to do" list than there are hours in the day, you feel stress.

According to a 2015 working paper by Harvard and Stanford Business schools, health problems associated with job-related anxiety (hypertension, cardiovascular disease, mental health) account for more deaths each year (120,000) than Alzheimer's disease, diabetes, or influenza. That is stunning. It's costing businesses a staggering amount of money, too. These stress-related health problems are blamed for $180 billion in annual healthcare expenses. That's a lot of money and a boatload of stress.

Stress, in low and brief doses, can be instrumental in getting us off the dime and set into motion. Excess or constant stress does a number on a host of things: our immune system, nervous system, cardiovascular system, and mental health.

It's our brain's fault, really.

Our amygdala (located in what some experts term our "downstairs brain") perceives threats and releases adrenaline. Adrenaline's job is to initiate an immediate reaction: to fight or flee. We get ourselves in deep trouble when we're jacked up with adrenaline in the middle of a staff meeting, though. As much as we might want to "throw hands" or run for the hills, our "upstairs brain," the one that can reason and pause to consider things more deeply, knows better. The bad news is that we are apt to run with our amygdala's invitation far too often, to our own (and others') detriment.

Why do we feel stress and anxiety when we feel rejected or when someone comes at us with contempt? It's brain chemistry again. Our primitive brain relied on social inclusion in order to survive. Rejection and contempt both threaten our survival; in response, these triggers stimulate stress hormones, cortisol, and adrenaline. Our bodies hold the increased anxiety, depression, and sadness at a chemical level.

The constant, elevated levels of stress are harmful to our physical and mental health. According to Wikipedia:

> Stress hormones such as cortisol and epinephrine are released by the body in situations that are interpreted as being potentially dangerous. Cortisol is believed to affect the metabolic system and epinephrine is believed to play a role in ADHD as well as depression and hypertension. Stress

hormones act by increasing heart rate, blood pressure, and breathing rate and shutting down metabolic processes such as digestion, reproduction, growth and immunity.

Like a car that's been running for days, eventually it runs out of gas and its systems start shutting down. Consistent stress tires the body, mind, and spirit. When we are stressed, we often regress to old, familiar patterns of behavior which usually aren't an example of our *best* behavior.

People with the best of intentions, skills, and habits can definitely go off the rails when the pressure won't let up. It's like a tea kettle: it needs to release steam, or heat needs to be cut, or it will literally explode. People are like tea kettles, my friend. We have breaking points and the scary thing is that you don't know what anyone's breaking point is in advance.

~ Violence ~

Some turn to violence when they reach their breaking point.

We are inundated in the news with evidence of pain creating more pain: mass and domestic violence, child abuse, sexual assault, and debilitating mental unwellness.

The United States has the highest violent crime rate of any industrialized nation. One in four (24%) women and one in seven (14%) men over 18 have been the victim of *severe* physical violence by an intimate partner in their lifetime (source: Centers for Disease Control & Prevention).

The most dangerous place for a woman to be is in her own home. One in four women experience domestic violence in their lifetime. Every nine SECONDS a woman in the United States is the victim of domestic violence. And what about the children ensconced in these dreadful situations? Just a couple of statistics boggle the mind. The United States is the worst among developed nations when it comes to how we treat our youngest, most innocent members. Four to seven children die from abuse every day. One in four girls (and one in six boys) will be sexually assaulted before they are eighteen.

Pain, and our failed attempts to release it, are destroying the fabric of our families and communities. We rely on relationships with others for our survival, but they can also influence our demise.

~ Things Are Getting Interesting ~

Dragging ourselves down, submerged in the pain, kills us from the inside out. Sending it outward threatens our relationships and the health of our families, communities, and workplaces.

Now that we know how our misuse of pain shows up in toxic ways within....and between....us, are you ready to investigate how we got tangled up in this mess in the first place? And how we can get out?

That's what I figured.

Key Chapter Concepts

- Our discomfort about feeling discomfort actually produces *more* of it.
- How we define events creates our experience of them, including our tendency to hold a narrative of suffering.
- That suffering perpetuates dynamics like repeating patterns, numbness, madness, and procrastination.
- Individuals, families, workplaces, communities, and societies are bearing pain's great burden...and circulating it 'round and 'round.

3

CRACKING THE CODE

"The reality you experience is a reflection of what you believe is most possible." ~ Bashar

I think we can all agree that Christopher Columbus wasn't a hero, our founding fathers weren't saintly, and fast food isn't good for us. The lies that supported those falsehoods have been disproven and exposed for what they were: comfortable illusions. Comfortable because they either benefitted someone or made us feel inspired or safe. Comfortable because they gave us a story we could rely on and didn't force us to reckon with *un*comfortable truths. Truth is often uncomfortable. It's messy. It's inconvenient. Facing the truth compels us to change: A belief, a mindset, a behavior. We resist change because change is scary. We know what we know and we feel in control of that knowledge. We like control. Change topples control, at least at first. So we resist change even when *not* changing is the worst possible thing for us.

Even when not changing means living with a lie; including the lies we tell ourselves to both avoid, or get trapped in, pain.

We think that when pain comes up, when a fear reveals itself, that this is perpetual, permanent. It's not. It's just a starting point...a call to awareness, to action…not a conviction or a sentence. It's a question mark, not a period. We profess to hate it, yet we hold it. Shoving it down. Blanketing ourselves in it. Shielding ourselves from it; in turn, becoming its prisoner, its **collector**.

In the keen words of Captain Jack Sparrow (from "Pirates of the Caribbean"): "The problem is not the problem. The problem is your *attitude* about the problem." And so it is with the "problem" of pain. Our problem with pain is not pain itself, it's how *we* perceive it. It's a lot like our issues with death. We think it's bad, tragic, the end; so, we are frightened of it, we deny it, we ignore its impending approach. Far too many of us live our days in its ominous shadow having never really *lived*. We've done pain a similar injustice. We avoid it, numb it, get lost in it, losing sight of its purpose, its value.

Pain is information. A sign. An invitation. It's also temporary. Inevitable. Unavoidable. Life isn't about avoiding pain; it's about not allowing it to drive the narrative of your life. It will continue to do that unless you see it for what it is.

~ Putting the Pieces in Place ~

Like a puzzle, to solve any problem, we must understand how it comes together. To fully understand it, we need to break it down into smaller parts. I'm going to do the very same thing with our pain problem, first telling you **why** we misunderstand it, then explaining **how** we misuse it.

What if I told you that what you've learned about pain is a lie? Here are some of the distortions and ways that pain gets a bad rap.

~ It's something we must avoid at all costs.

~ Once you have it, you're stuck with it.

~ Ignoring, pushing through, or burying it means you're strong.

~ You're too sensitive, or simply broken, if you feel a lot of it.

The people I've worked with have believed all of these lies at one time or another, sometimes all at once. Why? Well, these lies paint pain as bad, accumulating, oppressive, and even a piercing badge of honor. Because of this, they expend considerable energy avoiding it, muscling through it, and being judged by having it in the first place. In believing the lies, they think they're protecting themselves from hurt, from disappointment. If they fail before they start, then they won't be let down. If you're already on the ground, you can't fall.

The problem, of course, is that you're **on the ground**.

We were gaslit as children; told that our pain didn't matter, that our crying was an overreaction. That being sensitive was a bad thing. As a result, we deny our pain. Or we indulge it to prove it. To find validation.

What if I revealed the truth about pain? What if I shared new ways of understanding and processing it so we can release it? This chapter will share with you:

~ What pain does and doesn't do.

~ Where pain comes from.

~ What roles pain serves in our lives.

Like a good car mechanic, it doesn't help to jump in to fix something without determining what the real problem is first. Get ready to loosen your hold on your conceived notions about pain, those ideas that brought you to this moment but won't serve you well going forward.

Pain Rebel

~ Stop Complicating It ~

Humans have a tendency to complicate things. Even though the shortest distance between two points is a straight line, we find ourselves getting lost, running in circles on our way to being where we want to be. We get all twisted up with…omg, I'm doing it right now telling you about pain! See?

So, here goes. It's simple, really. Pain is a signal of two things:

1)   Something in the present is happening that's wrong, out of balance, not meeting your needs, etc.
2)   An old wound needs healing.

Hit your hand on a burner as you were cooking? That's number one. Stub your toe on the doorframe running for the microwave alarm? That's also number one. Searing headache from your kids (job, boyfriend, mother-in-law, dog, life)? Well, that's tougher to sort out. Why?

If your response to the event in question is proportionate, it's likely number one. Barking dogs can spur a headache. Screaming kids, same deal. Mother-in-law yammering on about some trivial nonsense, yup, twists those synapses into a clusterfuck brain squeeze.

If, on the other hand, your response to the situation is a bit overboard, then I'm guessing it's number two. How do you know if it's overboard or appropriate?

When my daughter was little, she was apt to respond dramatically to perceptibly small things. Given that she was my first born, it took me a second (shhhhh, yes, waaaaay longer than a true second) to figure out that she was likely one of three things: hot, hungry, or tired (number one signal). Once I'd triaged those triggers, I opted to see it as a "disproportionate response." Simply, this meant that how she was responding (tears, screams, etc.) was at a level higher than what was actually happening.

Talking her down off a ledge proved difficult until I chose to interpret her behavior not as wrong, but as too much of a good thing. It wasn't the FACT that she was upset that was disruptive; it was HOW upset she was getting.

Because I'm not a completely incompetent parent (note: I did say "completely" and didn't ask for confirmation from my teenagers), I explained it to my child this way (after she'd calmed down, of course, and had a snowball's chance in Hell of hearing me):

Scene: Screaming, stomping, throwing things on part of small child.

Me: You seem upset. On a scale of 1 to 5, how bad is what is happening? (Or, if she wasn't in a rating-things-kind-of-mood, "this situation looks like a 2, would you agree?")

Small child: Yes (muttered through adorable-yet-unsettling blubbering).

Me: This looks like a 4 or 5 reaction. The house wasn't burning down, right? So, we save our 5s for when something really, really awful is happening, right?

Small child: Yes (Note to self: Mom is a Jedi; I'll make a note to retaliate in my teens, for sure, once I figure out this "force" stuff.).

The difference between you and my daughter is that, well, we're not related, AND you're a grown-up so chances are, no one is doing this rating scale stuff with you.

If you're in pain, I'll wager a bet that you're known to overreact to any number of stimuli. You might explode, you might implode. But you're plode-ing. Why? All those drama queens (and kings) out there, listen up (Please. I know how *not* saying that might set you off and send you running): Do you see your reflection in this mirror I'm holding up? Do you find yourself operating like everything from a broken nail to a flat tire are 5s? Do people feel like they are walking on eggshells when you're around, trying not to upset you? Despite their attempts, they are rarely successful because, truth be told, you live in a state of upset. So, there's no distance to travel to get to that upset place because you're *always* there. Like a volcano, maybe it's obvious from a distance, maybe it's cloaked, but the lava is always there, ready to spill over. All it takes is a little shift in the ground and ba-BAM.

In the earlier example, my daughter hadn't yet regulated her responses to the world around her, so having a disproportionate response was simply a sign that she needed to learn about herself and the world around her. When you're all grown up and you've amassed bumps and bruises along the way and you find yourself having a response to a situation that's a 5 when it's by all accounts a 3, you're probably nursing some old wounds that need healing (helloooooo, number 2).

Note: It's a happy accident that I've named it number 2 since it refers to some old shit you're carrying around and it smells just as pretty.

But, before we can flush it, we need to learn a bit more about pain so we can deal with it honestly.

~ There Are Only Three Kinds of Pain ~

I admit that this seems oversimplistic, but it's quite true. Just because we overcomplicate something it doesn't mean that it isn't perfectly simple. I gravitate toward simple explanations because they make problems much easier to solve. And pain is the problem we're here to solve, right?

How We Take Our POWER Back

Pain comes from three places:

1. **Loss**
2. **Lack**
3. **Burden**

Loss refers to a longing for what we once had and don't have anymore.

Lack denotes a desire for something (or someone) we haven't acquired but want in our lives.

Burden equals a heaviness from something we don't want.

Since they both encompass not having what we want, **loss** (we had it once, but we don't have it anymore) and **lack** (we don't have it, and may never have had it) happen when we have unfulfilled needs, leaving us in a deficit position. Practically speaking, these could refer to a relationship, a physical or mental ability, job, or a financial situation. On the other hand, a **burden** puts us in a surplus position, but in a negative manner. It could be an injury or illness, or a situation exists that we don't want in our lives. When we've experienced trauma, this qualifies as a burden because we received what we didn't want.

~ The Three Time Periods of Pain ~

Time periods of pain, Dr. B? It's intuitive, really. There are three: Past, present, and future. Pain exists in all of them, each holding a different meaning and implication.

Past pain appears as regret or resentment, with a fixation on prior loss or trauma.

Present pain is being experienced in the moment we're in, with an appreciation for what *is* (versus what *was* or what *might be*).

Pain Rebel

Future pain shows up as fear, or obsession with events or circumstances that might happen but haven't happened yet.

~ *Trapped in the Past* ~

With **past** pain, we fail ourselves tragically reliving yesterday over and over again. Often centering around our core wound – that first, hard hit that leveled us – we get stuck in our stories, connected to our pain and those who hurt us. We filter what we see and hear through our wounds.

In reliving the pain, we keep the trauma alive. Bonded to those who hurt us, we pick up their swords and continue to martyr ourselves. What they did ended years ago, but we continue to pierce our spirits by brooding over the harm they inflicted. Our wounds are kept open and fresh, infected, and more tender as the years drag on. We tie not only our pasts to the bad behavior of others, but we do the same to our present and our future. We hand over the pen to our own story by letting the actions and beliefs of others define us. We deny our own truth; create a rift in our relationship with ourselves by adopting their skewed, self-interested, broken perceptions and agendas.

What if I told you that your bond to the pain was actually loyalty?

Now, the last thing you probably consider yourself is loyal to those who hurt you long ago, am I right? Loyalty means that you are allowing what they did to continue to hurt you, or, embracing their hurtful, limiting beliefs about you. In either case, you are giving them power not only over yesterday, but *today* (and most likely, *tomorrow*).

We can only properly heal yesterday by cutting our attachment to those events. Then and only then can we experience today. Past pain has a useful purpose: To learn so we can grow. Holding onto to past hurts is a habit we can break, because that's what it is: a habit.

~ *Future Fear* ~

With **future** pain, we get locked into fear about an unknown future, an anticipatory loss or burden. We fear heartbreak, so we stay wedded to our sense of control to reduce the risk that we'll ever be hurt again.

Instead of being protected from pain, what we end up with is a dull heartache, a perpetual reminder to be careful. We do anything to avoid pain, yet we're steeped in it. We feel pain in anticipation of an uncertain future, all informed by our past experiences and expectations about what's likely to happen. We tend to live our lives in perpetual anticipation, never stopping long enough to actually LIVE it.

Inside your head is fantasy and hypotheticals. Outside your head is reality, what's actually happening around you. Many of us carry our ideas about an unknown future in our little world inside our heads. We take action...but *fantasy* action. We're *thinking* about all the things we want, yet we aren't *doing* anything in real life about creating that future.

We're living in a future that we haven't reached and throwing away the moment we're actually occupying.

If we've been hurt in love, we might believe that people are stupid, careless, and self-focused. Love gets sidelined when you focus on the rejection we expect to arrive. You're bound to feel unworthy when your self-concept is pinned to the whims of others. Ohhhh, it feels tremendous when they are paying attention and doting on you. Not so much when they forget about you. To protect ourselves, we hold fear close.

Fear has a better purpose, of course.

Fear is quite helpful when you use IT with intention not when you let it use YOU out of unchallenged patterning (you know, the automatic responses you have that you've yet to pause to assess and change because maybe they don't serve you?).

Fear, properly used, is an early warning system. It tells you that a train might be headed down the track with you in its path. It invites you to consider your options, to make a plan. We wouldn't have survived this long as a species if we hadn't listened to fear. LISTEN to it. Just don't OPERATE from it. Which brings us to the **present**...

~ *The Present of the Present* ~

Real, useful pain only exists in the **present** moment.

When we confront a painful situation in the present, our minds aren't usually the first dogs in the fight. Freeze (or fight, flight, or even fawn) is our body's initial, reactive survival-mode response to **present** pain. Unfortunately, it's even more deeply automatic if it's rooted in trauma. Not surprisingly, trauma kicks off a knee-jerk response to triggers, particularly familiar ones. No one wants to go through another trauma, so your body protects you by launching into autopilot.

But remember, you have more than one brain governing your responses. Your "downstairs brain" (limbic system) can be overridden by your "upstairs brain" (your pre-frontal cortex). You have the power to move past your initial fear. To acknowledge it, honor it, and then release it. Remind yourself that this is *now*. This is not *always*. This has not always been here so this will not always be here. It's okay to feel crappy when crappy things happen. You also know that whatever is happening in this moment won't last long. Feel it while it's here and then let it go.

How We Take Our POWER Back

If we don't, our cumulative injuries become the:
~ Crosses we hang ourselves on
~ Shrouds/walls we hide behind
~ Swords we punish others with

None of these pains are from new, **present** injuries. They are simply being experienced in the present because we carried them here. In effect, we time traveled to grab something from the past to ruminate over or catapulted ourselves into the future to obsess over what might be in store for us. In doing so, we find ourselves living in regret (living in past pain), or fear (consumed by possible future pain).

That said, sometimes we must escape the present moment so as to lessen the depth of a painful event. That's a respectable survival tactic. Time travel can be self-protective, *as long as we return* to do the work to learn from and release it. Our power exists only in the present. Stay in it.

Think of when you have a fever; you look for the underlying illness, don't you? Acknowledging your cumulative injuries, or "collections," points you in a healing direction. Do you want to be in pain? I'm sure you said, "no (fucking) way!" Yet, our actions reveal something else. In truth, we hold fast to our psychic pain, devoting our lives to clinging to it and manifesting it over and over again on new stages with new actors.

Think of the music we listen to. Sure, there are plenty of happy, romantic ballads and upbeat, inspiring tunes. Yet, the vast majority of songs are about pain, loss, anger, and retaliation. Our music reinforces the bill of goods we were sold that life and love are painful. How many times have you been in the car or hanging with friends and belted out a ballad in tribute to someone who broke your heart in one way or another? When have you indulged that ache until you felt like it might swallow you whole? Too often, we define ourselves by our losses, a practice which keeps them present and persistent and wholly *expected*. There IS another way.

Pain Rebel

"Whatever the present moment contains,
accept it as if you had chosen it." ~ Eckart Tolle

~ Roles Holding Pain Serves ~

You've likely gotten the impression that I believe that holding onto pain is terrible. That being a Pain Collector is all bad. Over decades of working with people to improve their lives, I've found a clear truth: If you don't acknowledge the good that a "bad" thing does, you'll never let go of it and its benefits.

So here's the truth: There **are** roles that holding pain serves. There are ways that it comforts, protects, connects, and punishes. Defense mechanisms of sorts, these roles allow us to withstand pain until we figure out or decide how we'd like to process and release it. Think of these roles as idling in traffic. Before you get to your destination, you'll be sitting at a few traffic lights. You might sit at a fork in the road for a bit, deciding which way to go, but you don't *stay* there. The same is true for these roles for pain in your journey.

Comforter. Acknowledges and indulges our pain. Telling us that we matter and that we are worthy of empathy and soothing.

Protector. Keeps people, experiences, risks away so we don't get hurt again. Serves as the great insulator.

Connector. We all love to bitch, moan, and complain. It joins us with others by finding common enemies to commiserate about.

Punisher. Also called the "prosecutor." This role reminds us and tells others how something hurt and seeks to attack others who injured us.

Looking at the chart below, each role differs in its bend towards compassion or aggression and internal versus external focus. One note: The interesting practice of the Punisher is that while its focus is on the external, it also internalizes its sentence. We may persecute others for what we perceive they've done to us while still punishing ourselves for mistakes we've made.

	Internal Focus	External Focus
Aggression	**PROTECTOR** (insulate)	**PUNISHER** (attack)
Compassion	**COMFORTER** (indulge)	**CONNECTOR** (commiserate)

Which role resonates with you? To see how each role might take hold in your life, reflect on your answers to the following questions.

Comforter: Do you think about the ways you've been hurt and see these injuries as the reasons why you struggle now? Do you console yourself with the stories of hurts you've experienced, often using those stories as the rationale for your current lot in life?

Protector: Do you think about how others are likely to hurt you and that you need to take measures to prevent that from happening? Do your stories keep you from taking relationship risks because you know ahead of time how people are likely to hurt you?

Connector: Do you share your troubles (past and present) with others and feel better when they acknowledge your pain and perhaps also share their own? Does your pain gain you favor with those around you, perhaps because you being happy wouldn't fit in?

Punisher: Do you hold grudges against people (or populations like men, women, bosses, authority) based on your past injuries?

Clearly, these aren't bad things in and of themselves. The toxicity sets in when you get stuck in one or more of these roles, seeing them as the end point in your healing process instead of a pitstop. Don't fire these players, just place them on temporary assignment.

"Everything changes once we identify with being the witness to the story, instead of the actor in it." ~ Ram Dass

~ Behind the Mask ~

We've looked at where pain comes from, what it does and doesn't do, and what its roles often are. Now it's time to see what its true purposes are. Properly used, pain is our informant, teacher, and guide.

Pain *informs* us that something is out of balance, needing attention, soothing, or healing.

Pain *teaches* us things about ourselves and one another.

Pain *guides* us, through our healing, to a better way of living.

It helps us answer the following questions:

~ Where is it coming from?
~ Why is it familiar?
~ What is it trying to tell me?
~ How can I honor it?

Pain Rebels believe that things are happening **for** us, not **to** us. We see that circumstances, even painful ones, allow us to be better for them having happened. So pain isn't our captor; it's something bigger and better if we permit ourselves to be its student. We stop pushing against it and instead reserve our energy for addressing the learning and healing that it invites.

Pain Rebels accept that life is messy. We see the purpose of life as learning and growing, shifting us from being fixated only on outcomes. The journey *is* the destination. This mindset shift lifts the pressure we've put on ourselves and others to be perfect and life to be tidy. Pain Rebels don't waste energy on bending the world to our will. As a result, we feel less emotion when our plan goes off course. We know we can handle whatever the world throws at us and keep going.

~ Onto Better Days ~

Now that we better understand pain, we can move forward to create new neural pathways in our brains, shaping what life is and how it can be. Stuck in our old ways of thinking will only produce more of the same experiences of life. If you want a better life, prepare to allow your thoughts to be shifted. It's not easy, but it is pretty simple. Entertain a new thought and watch the world unfold before you.

Key Chapter Concepts

- We've been believing lies about pain.
- How we see pain equals how we experience it.
- There are three kinds of pain: loss, lack, and burden.
- There are three time periods of pain: past, present, and future.
- Pain serves us: Protector, Punisher, Comforter, and Connector.

"People have a hard time letting go of their suffering.
Out of fear of the unknown, they prefer
suffering that is familiar." ~ Thich Nhat Hanh

4

CHANGE SUCKS

Yeah, I said it. Change sucks. And it's exactly why you might reject my proposition to become a Pain Rebel. The devil you know is better than the one you don't, right?

You should know that I'm taking a great risk saying so since I get paid to help people manifest change. But I pull no punches and I won't disrespect you by lying to you and pretending that change is unicorns dancing in rainbows. It's not. It's hard work sometimes. It can even be excruciating. Why is change so hard and what makes one change only slightly painful and another torturous?

A tricky little thing called Ego. Ego also goes by the nickname, "Will." For the sake of ease, I'll refer to Will as "he" (vs. "she") from here on out.

He's a force to be reckoned with, for sure. He gets a bad rap for being self-centered and all, but his real Achilles heel is that he needs to be in control at all costs. Control is a dirty word for some, but I've yet to meet anyone who doesn't like to be in control. Maybe not dictator-level control, but control, nonetheless. Control makes us feel safe. Will likes to feel safe (and right).

Change messes up all of that. Even the scent of change in the distance can get Will all worked up and putting on quite a show. He wants to tell everyone why it won't work or why it's not necessary. He wants to derail it, even if on the surface he's "supporting" it because it threatens his safe haven of sameness.

We all have a little Will in us. We crave sameness and predictability because it makes us feel safe and in control. Change doesn't offer guarantees. The grass on the other side of the fence looks great but making the change means taking a chance on less than a sure thing. I can't tell you how many organizations and individuals have engaged my services to embark on a great change journey only to jump ship when things started to get uncomfortable.

~ Resistance ~

Living in New England we have a saying, "if you're bored with the weather just wait a minute." Our scorching hot and humid summer days are equaled only by our frigid winter nights. One such night I was walking my rambunctious dog in my neighborhood and realized I'd underdressed for the occasion. As the shivers set in, I started thinking about this book, pain. About how I was experiencing that moment. About how my perception of cold and what it was supposed to feel like was creating my experience. We view cold as suffering. When we see someone out, like I was that dark, winter night, we ask, "aren't you COLD?" Cold is simply one of many human sensations. It can be listened to. Appreciated. Ignored. Resisted. Pain exists in resistance. That's where our attention is directed. We reinforce and strengthen its hold by perceiving it as bad and fighting it.

I love how trees look in the dead of winter. Bare, naked, and so very different from just weeks before. When it's full and cloaked with leaves, it's stunning and appears bountiful, abundant, and perfect. When bare, you witness its stunted, broken, imperfect branches and form, its misshapen structure. Its fragility. The very same things that provide its unique beauty when full are revealed when you remove its covering and see its imperfections.

Like us, trees are perfectly imperfect and ever-changing. Trying to stop leaves from changing is just as futile as trying to resist the changes required to benefit us.

Why do we fundamentally resist change, even when we are surrounded by darkness? It often comes down to one simple word:

Grief.

In order to (properly) change, we must grieve what *was* in order to latch onto what *is*.

Deep, lasting change is anchored in grief work. "Grief work" doesn't mean diving into a rabbit hole of sorrow and regret. It means taking stock of where we were in order to buy into where we are going. So much of what we've been doing up to this point we've been woefully unaware of.

One surefire way to kick this awareness thing into full gear is to examine how our patterns keep showing up again and again. Maybe then we'll be convinced the change isn't so bad after all…

~ Déjà Vu-Ville ~

I could have called this, "How Did I Get HERE again?" If you find yourself in one bad relationship, job, or circumstance over and over (and over) again, listen up. Pain keeps showing up in your life in a similar way time after time for a reason. I liken it to the game, "Whack-a-Mole;" every time you push one problem or pain out, another surfaces…in a modified form or through a different person, relationship, job, or situation.

How We Take Our POWER Back

One of my favorite lines from a series I used to love, "Sex and the City," was from Carrie Bradshaw's therapist: In discussing the line of failed relationships in Carrie's past, she said, "What do all of these men have in common? *You.*" Ouch.

If you're an awakened soul, you've likely noticed this pattern and resolved to break it, to no avail. The story you tell yourself might predict a lifetime of repeating the past, caught in a cycle you feel powerless to break. If these were good patterns, we'd boast about the life lottery we keep winning. Unfortunately, that's rarely the case. Our life keeps hitting the guardrails and we are at our wits' end. If this were a job, we'd have given our notice years ago.

What gives?

Well, you are stuck in a position, you just didn't remember taking the job.

~ Pain Resumés ~

If you're over the age of 22, you've surely constructed a resumé, chronicling your skills, knowledge, and experiences. The same holds true for a *pain resumé*. Pain resumés are how we recount our burning experiences to validate who and where we are. Think of the last time you got into a new relationship (romantic or platonic) and started telling each other stories about who you are and where you came from. These stories...the painful ones...constitute your pain resumé.

Too often, we indulge our pain to prove its existence...and our worth... to others. It's like we're on a megaphone screaming,

"LOOK AT ME AND HOW MUCH PAIN I'M IN!"

We want to be SEEN. Acknowledged. Validated. Unlike a broken leg, no one can see how hurt we are on the inside unless we tell them. So, what do we do? We show off our internal scars. We say, "This is what happened to ME. This is what explains why I need, do, want, feel THIS."

The more we tell the story, the more we suffer. Have you known people who could quickly recount every bad hand they were dealt? Me, too. I was raised by two of them.

Speaking of these injured parties, let's take a look-see at what my father's looked like, shall we? I mean, he never wrote one, but BOY he lived it.

My Dad's Pain Resumé (in his voice)

My father left before I was born. I was born and grew up poor.

My mother was strict and aloof.

As a child and young adult, I was overweight and kids made fun of me.

Unlike my siblings, I had red hair and freckles, standing out like a sore thumb.

I got injured after joining the military at nineteen, developing a blood-clotting disorder and have been in daily pain ever since. I became disabled, and suffered numerous heart attacks, pulmonary embolism and a stroke before I was 22.

I'm now a drug addict, criminal, womanizer, domestic abuser, failure, and feel unlovable and unredeemable.

In my dad's case, it's not surprising that he lived the life of a Pain Collector. When you share the ugly stories to the exclusion of the pleasurable ones, when you fail to see how that pain can serve your present joy, that's when it's adding to your Pain Collector status. The same held true for my dad. He gathered more and more pain and shelled it out to others.

Tragically, he couldn't see that the alternative, that living a life of joy and opportunity was to write a *different* resumé: I call it Pain's *Potential* Resumé. Instead of seeing only the pain of those moments and circumstances, he would have defined those events as to how they spurred his positive response; how he used them to make his life better. It would depict the *potential* good he could have done in the world if only he could have seen how pain could *serve* instead of *destroy* him. How might this new and improved resumé have looked?

Dad's Pain's *Potential* Resumé (in his imagined voice)

My father left before I was born. I was born poor. I vowed to make things better for me, and for my daughter. I stayed in her life and provided for her in ways he never provided for me.

My mother was strict and aloof. I knew the pain of that, so I was firm, but warm, with my own child.

As a child and young adult, I was overweight and kids made fun of me. This made me sensitive to how others perceive themselves and I learned to accept myself as I am and help others do the same.

Unlike my siblings, I had red hair and freckles, standing out like a sore thumb. Being different from my family allowed me freedom from growing up like them.

I got injured after joining the military at nineteen, developing a blood-clotting disorder and have been in daily pain ever since. I became disabled, suffered numerous heart attacks, pulmonary embolisms, and a stroke before age 22. I took my health issues seriously and didn't make things worse through my own choices.

Pain Rebel

I'm now an artist and poet. I am generous with my time and my experience. I mentor others who are recovering addicts. I'm a health advocate for those who have contracted illnesses early on and as part of their military service. I vowed to be different so I am. I do things in the world *because* of my painful upbringing, not in spite of it.

It's never too late to rewrite your resumé. You can look back to see the gifts and lessons and use them to inform your new identity. Now, the truth is that the longer he held his early hurts, the harder it became to recraft a narrative as hero versus victim. How long have you been holding onto yours? Every day you wait to rewrite it is another day lost to the magic you could bring to the world.

Mourn the time you spent in that dead-end job and accept this invitation to start a new one of your own design. Sure, it sucks big time that you spent countless years repeating patterns that delivered copious amounts of pain. It's no small wonder if you're grief-stricken.

Fortunately, we can learn a lot about how different cultures mourn. Whether it's hosting crying circles or sitting Shiva, some groups welcome feeling the feelings when they come. Too many of us have accepted the flawed notion that we must numb out **or** fall apart. We panic, so we deny our aching. Our grief goes underground, habitually showing up in mental instability, unhealthy eating and/or working, and full-blown addictions.

The safe and sane resolution? Commit to doing this differently. Resist the tried and true. Put down the Ben & Jerry's quart and face the loss of your go-to tactics. They got you here; if you want to be "there," you'll need to walk a different path. Know this: It's not going to be easy. It's going to be downright uncomfortable. It might even be terrifying to sit in the space between what you've always known and what you haven't yet experienced. You're straddling two worlds and you must choose.

How We Take Our POWER Back

~ The Change Solution ~

What do we do? Stay where we are? Plant ourselves firmly in the mud and muck of our current state? No freaking way. Life is too short and the experiences we miss by maintaining the status quo (especially when it involves a crazy level of dysfunction and drama) aren't coming back. They are gone. Time passes. Opportunities skate by. What's that old adage? We don't regret the things we did nearly as much as the things we failed to do.

DO.

To really DO, you simply need a game plan to negotiate with Will. This book IS your game plan. Because, do you want the good news?

We can change. And when *we* change, the *situation* changes.

~ Move from Pain Collector to Pain Rebel ~

We can change through adopting new practices due to something called "brain plasticity." Brain plasticity, simply put, is our ability to adapt our brains to new information, habits, and experiences no matter how old we are.

We accumulate injuries along the road of life, each building on the collective "last." Using every similar experience to stay stuck in not changing because each subsequent experience "confirms" our internal script about pain. In order to experience and process each encounter with honesty, fairness, optimal health, and balanced perspective, we have to unpack and release the string of collective hurts.

Trauma creates pain. As we reviewed earlier in the book, pain held in becomes self-injury and destruction. It shows up as depression, anxiety, and, too often, suicide, slow or sudden. Pain sent outward becomes rage and violence. It shows us as bullying, intimate partner violence, and even mass murder.

Me? I swallowed it and it almost swallowed me. I know first-hand that we drown not by falling into the water...we drown by staying submerged in it. Once we are back on the shore, we must find a way to change our futures. We do this by compassionately and powerfully honoring our pasts. Honoring them by refusing to be owned by them.

We repeat that which we do not resolve.

To resolve it, we have to do the work. I learned how to set myself free and I desperately want to share my path...*your* path...with you. This book is what I mean by "do the work." Believe me, if you follow the guidance of "Pain Rebel," the lightening of the baggage you've been hauling around **will** occur.

"Pain Rebel" is a guide for thriving in a cold, cruel world (that really isn't so cold or cruel). In this short, sweet, bitter life, we take the good with the bad. We seek the good wrapped up inside the bad and discover the bad concealed in the good. We honor that the bad beckons our growth. In order to grow, we must stop wasting today in the shadows of yesterdays. We must take what drags us down and transform it into what drives us up. We must rise above our tragedies. If we haven't found a hero, why not become our own hero! You can save your own damn self.

It's time.

Honestly, it's your choice: Will it be door number one or door number two?

Behind door number one stands the tried and true, Pain Collector, holding denial close, often careening through life, asleep at the wheel. The Pain Collector's heart is filled with rage...or sorrow...locked in a fight...or resigned to defeat.

PAIN COLLECTOR

Behind door number two stands a new friend, the Pain Rebel, living life large, boldly, awakened to all the ups and downs that life promises. The Pain Rebel, strengthened by raised awareness and intention, has a heart that is bursting with acceptance, love, and power.

PAIN REBEL

The Pain Rebel knows full well that resisting pain creates exhaustion and misery. Allowing it manifests authenticity and healing. You see, although things are *painful*, most are not *lethal*. We must remind ourselves that what is painful is rarely lethal. That this won't kill me, this will pain me. There is a difference. Our power lies in the difference. Pain can (and will) come and go…if you don't push it down or hang onto it. Pain multiplies in the fight and avoidance. Fight the right fight: the one where you fight to become a Pain Rebel.

Ready to rumble?

"One day or day one. You decide." ~*Paulo Coelho*

5

GETTING READY

Any good rebel needs resources to support them when the nights are long and the road is dim.

Below are five actions that will support your shifts in your thinking and feeling, and solidify your Pain Rebel status through behavior changes.

1. **Journaling.** This practice helps you to process what's happening and offers a brain dump so you can free up some mental space for more useful things. People who journal have a greater rate and depth of recovery, visit the doctor less, and I contend that I'd find them with more power. Getting things out of your head and on paper allows you to review what you've been thinking and feeling. As you know from this change process so far, identifying what you're thinking and where it might be "off" allows you to shift your thinking and then adjust how you feel. When you feel differently, you behave differently. Want to change your path? Journal. How do you journal? There are as many ways to journal as there are people, and there are even apps for doing it. Whatever is troubling you, write about it. Since the intention is to elevate your awareness of how you think and feel in order to expand your choices as to how to behave, simply ask yourself "How am I

thinking about this?" or "How am I feeling about this?" Use the prompts in this book as starting points to stretch that awareness muscle. Then, get writing.

2. **Talking About It:** Let me be crystal clear. Talking about an issue is *not* a replacement for doing something about it, but it can act as a catalyst and an accountability step. Much like writing things down, talking about them makes them real. Having a goal in secret is one thing: Sharing it with the world makes it real and holds you accountable to others. Share it and you'll nail it. Telling other people what you're struggling through is a public pronouncement, as well, so there is inherent accountability, potential validation and support, and challenge. When you share your thoughts with another person (no, your dog doesn't count), you can welcome in new perspectives and suggestions on how to shift your thinking. One important point: Don't just share things with a person who is your mental twin, who thinks about things the same way that you do. Clearly, this might serve to validate you, but it won't challenge your assumptions. If you're in it to win it in the change department, branch out and share your struggle with someone who might (gasp!) disagree with you.

3. **Just Do It:** I've coached countless people over the years and the vast proportion of them dealt with anxiety about making a move in the right direction. They got stuck because they stopped moving. Get it? It's only possible to get stuck if you're not in motion. Put yourself in motion. When in doubt, act. I mean that literally. Take one small step toward the change you want by pretending that you're just playing a role, acting a part. If your mind is your enemy, make your body your friend. If you don't "feel" like going to the gym, go. Your mind will catch up. This is one way in which the thoughts-feelings-behaviors chain doesn't necessarily apply. If your thoughts and feelings are getting in your way and you're stuck, move first. Move a little, move a lot. Just *move.*

4. **Get a Partner:** Misery loves company and so does change. When you want to get in shape, get a workout buddy who keeps you honest. Group weight loss systems are popular for the same reason. Have a change you want to tackle? Find a friend or co-worker who is up for their own challenge (doesn't have to be the same trait or behavior, and it often works better if they are different) and form an accountability team. Check in daily or weekly, depending on the change. Celebrate your strides, nudge each other along during your slips. Build a network of friends, family, colleagues, and contacts to call upon for when you need this sort of partnership. Hire a coach (yes, you can call yours truly!). Nothing knocks you off balance like thinking or feeling like you're all alone, a one-man/woman show. You're not.

5. **Establish a Reward System:** You can combine this one with some of the other tactics on this list. Admit it, you're like a dog. Yes, you. You want to get a cookie when you've done something well. Use your natural drive for validation by setting up rewards ("coooooooookies") when you practice certain skills or reach certain milestones. Maybe it's a present to yourself of material goods, a treat, or time off or away. If you're a friend, partner, parent, or employer, remember that we all have a need for acknowledgment and appreciation. To be caught doing something right. Sometimes we get so caught up in correcting and "guiding" that we forget how important it is to tell someone that we see the good they did. To throw them a cookie. Just a cookie. Not a platter, especially if they are screwing up more than they are succeeding. But a cookie. Just to give them a taste of the reward that we all hunger for. You'll soon find that they feel encouraged to be better so they can "earn" more.

As you can see, modifying your behavior is not nearly as complicated as modifying your thoughts and feelings. Sometimes making a change to how you act is just that, an act. Fake it till you make it, as my aunt always tells me. Along the way to making it, you'll start believing that the faking it isn't so fake after all.

Now that we've covered some no-brainers for changing your behaviors, it's time to dig deeper and fill up your toolbox of options to get the change you desire.

6

BREAKING PATTERNS

"Strength shows not only in the ability to persist, but in the ability to start over." ~ F. Scott Fitzgerald

Helloooooo! Welcome to your caffeinated, jumpstart, alarm clock buzzer of a wake-up call. If you're anything like the vast majority of people out there, you've been asleep at the wheel on one or more roads of your life. Maybe it was just a short cul-de-sac. Perhaps it was a long, winding country road. It might hae been every highway and byway until an event or person jolted you awake.

Your eyes are now open. You know you want "things" to be different, even if you haven't the slightest clue as to what those things are or how to proceed. That's okay! You're holding the manual to bring you there. You're not alone. You're supported. You have resources and a trained guide to bring you across the bridge of where you've been floundering, suffering, to where you'll prosper.

You moved through the ickiest part of this book: A thorough and depressing play-by-play of the problem and symptoms of a Pain Collector's journey. Before you got lost in the bad news, you grabbed the life raft of the solution and now you're diving into the first step in your transformational journey. This journey will not be easy; there are no quick fixes to this, but I will walk you through the process. You got here; you can get out.

I know, it's scary. I get it. I've been exactly where you are more than once. Yeah, the path of a Pain Rebel is not a straight one, at least not usually. We Pain Rebels get caught up in our own heartbreaking reenactments, revisiting old wounds and patterns. Once you sign up to live as a Pain Rebel, though, you commit to letting things come and go, moving through you, not taking hold of you. When you find yourself in those similar, uncomfortable situations, you tap into the first step of the change process to reclaim your power: Awareness.

Knowledge is power. When you can see what's going on, you're one step closer to healing. Like lighting a candle in a power outage, you're safer and have more options when you can see what's happening around you. The Awareness step is simply a candle for your outsides *and* your insides. For the patterns and relationships encircling you as well as the disruptions in your head and heart. When you know something is wrong you can make a decision to fix it. If not, you're just cruising on down the road, risking an engine blowout or leaving a trail of toxic smoke.

Bottom line: You are now acutely aware that you've been operating on less than full power. Why? Let's find out by tackling the next step: Assessment.

~ Finding Authenticity ~

When I dig into the psyches of my clients, I find two big fears: Being a failure and being found out to be a fraud. An entangled mess, both fears are rooted in expectations. Before you could decide for yourself what you wanted, needed, and found acceptable, you subconsciously agreed to someone else's version of how things were and were supposed to be. At some level, you've always sensed that you were living differently than you wanted to, thinking about yourself in ways that weren't pure to who you were intended to be. Buried in your subconscious is this juxtaposition of what your spirit knows and how you're thinking and acting.

It's no wonder that the imposter syndrome pops up! Having the fear of being found out to be a fraud may be rooted in a lack of authenticity at such a core level. Your subconscious is calling you out, bringing your attention to your disingenuousness. It may have nothing to do with your inability to succeed, but, instead, your unwillingness to live your truth. Your subconscious isn't telling you that you're *un*worthy…it's screaming out that you are *more* worthy than you're giving yourself credit for.

In short, you have a fraud *friend.* Your fraud friend wants you to knock off your bullshit by examining and rewriting the narrative of your life so you can live how you were *meant* to live…heroically, but not locked in a war with ourselves.

It's said that most of us battle with our weight. We want to be thin, fit, and healthy but find ourselves overweight and flabby. We want to **be** different, but we don't **act** differently. We see all the options open to us but don't commit to any of them. We make a New Year's resolution to drop fifteen pounds but stop going to the gym by March, if not sooner.

Why?

Well, it's typically not laziness. Or that we don't want to have the result. It's that we don't know how to navigate the process successfully, so we lose hope and commitment. We are experts at establishing patterns, not breaking them. What are we missing?

We fail to comprehend our resistance. We've found ways to stay stuck and those conditioned responses don't just disappear when we commit to wanting to be where we aren't. We resist turning over a new leaf because there's a payoff in our pain. What?

~ Coping Mechanisms Aren't All Bad ~

To break a pattern, we need to acknowledge how it serves us, even if it seems destructive. Coping mechanisms can be damaging, but they are also quite useful. They help us cope. One of the most popular ones is distraction. Distractions aren't inherently bad. Distractions serve as a temporary adaptation to float above and pull away from pain. Examples of distractions include new relationships, bad habits, work, fads and diets, social media, etc.

Distractions can save us when we aren't prepared to save ourselves. One workshop attendee of mine unimaginably lost her infant child and her parent in the same month. She used her grief to mobilize her purpose to knock it out of the park professionally. She dove head-first into work and became relentless and hyper-focused. It helped her to compartmentalize her pain while simultaneously serving her need for control. We often numb until we can do the work necessary to clear the pain…to sort it out. Because remember:

They are COPING mechanisms not HEALING mechanisms. Coping mechanisms help us *survive*; healing mechanisms help us *thrive*.

Let's get onto the healing and thriving, shall we?

~ Assessing Lessons from the Past ~

Leaving the past in the past is a terrific adage but it doesn't do you any good if you haven't already learned from your past before you put it to rest. It's critical to take a brief look back at your life so you can recognize patterns that may or may not be serving you as you embark on a path of change.

Right after my dad died when I was 24, I found a t-shirt that read "when life gives you scraps, make a quilt." I bought it on the spot and wore that with pride for many months. Since I don't know you, I don't know if you've had a tough go of it, or if your life has been a cakewalk. I'd wager that even if by some accounts you've had it fairly easy, we all get bumped and bruised along the way. What do your scraps look like? I really do try to live by the tenet that it's not what happens to you, but how you handle what happens to you, that matters.

Are you ready to put that into play? To make the best of what's happened in your life? Then it's time to tackle some assessment...to interview yourself so you can get a handle on how you're allowing your negative past experiences to affect you today.

What are the worst things that have ever happened in your life?

1.

2.

3.

What lessons about the world (and yourself) did you learn from these experiences?

1.

2.

3.

When have you had to revisit these lessons because history seemed to repeat itself? Did you realize that you were in a déjà vu moment right away or did it take you some time to figure it out?

Do you feel stronger or weaker as a result of these hard times? Explain.

I have an e-mail subscription to "Notes from the Universe™" (thanks, Mike Dooley!) which means that I get daily inspiration about my potential and the abundance of the Universe. One of the underlying principles of these notes is that we have control over our destinies through our thoughts and making deliberate actions toward the life we want for ourselves. The Notes from the Universe™ tell us that "thoughts become things," so if we can master our thoughts, we can master occurrences. If that's true, then we are in control of our thoughts AND external events. I disagree. We *influence* them strongly, but we have to focus on our influence *not* on the <u>outcome</u> because the sheer chaos of the universe dictates that we have *influence* but not *control*. We are not puppet masters. Stuff happens. It's what we do in response to the "stuff" that defines who we are, our happiness level, and our success (however we choose to define that).

~ Assessing Your Current State ~

Conducting an interview with yourself hopefully brought forth some eye-opening observations about where you've traveled to this point in your life. Now it's time to assess where you are today. Today is really just a culmination of every yesterday: The decisions you made brought you to today. So, where are you? Let's investigate.

Describe your worldview as it is today. What do you believe about yourself and the world around you? Is the world benevolent, flawed, or doomed?

Now, give me three words and three words only, to summarize your state of mind right now. Not how you *wish it would be*; how it really *is* right at this very moment.

1.

2.

3.

What don't you like about where you are right now? Where would you direct a magic wand if I handed you one? What situation, relationship, or mindset would you change?

What are you angry at? What are you sad or disappointed about?

What are the things you're accepting in your life that make you resentful, stressed out, angry, sad, or just generally unfulfilled? It might be a relationship or a habit.

Pain Rebel

What are you struggling to accept about your current reality?

What do you want to rebel from?

What do you want to release? Maybe it's a relationship or a burden you feel or shame you've been carrying or resentments you've been holding.

What do you have to grieve about your path to this point, how you got here? Is there an old way of being or a relationship or a belief you have about yourself that's holding you back from making things different?

What do you want to forgive, to break away from, to be free from?

You cannot grow if you continue to treat yourself in unhealthy ways, whether you've "hired" someone else to do it (by being in a destructive relationship) or you're doing it yourself. What can you agree to do going forward to treat yourself in healthy ways? Get creative. How can you best show love to yourself?

~ Time Periods of Pain Revisited ~

A couple of chapters ago, we separated pain into time periods: past, present, and future. We drag past pain into the present and future. We worry about future events based in fear of a moment that hasn't happened…and may never happen. Doing so takes away our power today. It's said that 50% of our day is spent thinking about things that are out of our control and beyond our immediate environment. Half! Talk about a loss of power!

As a Pain Rebel, what can we do?

Acknowledge it, comfort it (self-soothing measures), then take action. DO something. Harness your anxious energy toward something positive: Action.

When you feel fear or dread (future-focused), you can get lost in the "what ifs" or you can use them to your advantage. Something bad happens, or hasn't yet happened, and you're lost in a manic, circular spin of what ifs. What if this? What if that? What if this then that then this then that? You can "what if?" yourself right into the funny farm. When I tackled this with a client she remarked, "the 'What If' Monster and I are *besties*!"

What if (I know, ironic to start this way, but hang with me) I told you that this monster really *was* your very best friend, your protector? That it's all part of a warning system designed to protect you from harm. Feeling panic isn't the enemy. It's the limbic system in your brain seeing if you need to fight, flee, or freeze. What you *do with it,* how you seize that opportunity, is the crucial part.

How do you move from panic mode to problem solver? First, understand that panic mode is simply a steppingstone to a power position. It helps us to plan and planning keeps us safe. Sure, you could not freak out in the first place and just skip that irritatingly paralyzing step, but what's the fun in *that?* When your limbic system is activated, you can't help but notice that something might be wrong. Identifying a problem is the first necessary step to solving it. The trick is not to become immobilized by the what ifs.

In my bulimic phase, I could scarf down three boxes (not bowls, BOXES) of cookies with a half-gallon milk chaser. Once I opened a box, I got lost in shoving cookie after cookie in my mouth. These episodes would take less than an hour, but the damage lasted much longer. Fast forward thirty years. Do I eat cookies? Yes. Do I eat a box (or boxes) at a time? No. Through my healing process, I recognized that I was capable of eating a reasonable, healthy portion of just few cookies. The thought of cookies no longer fills me with panic that I am going to fall off the eating-disorder-cliff.

The secret to my recovery was to get my behavior to rise to the level of choice. In the midst of your "what if" obsession, just "eat" a couple before you reseal the box. To take your power back, simply ask yourself, "If this next 'what if' is true, what is the first problem I can solve?" Harness your anxious energy into movement; movement toward solving the next problem. Then the problem after that, and the problem after that. Before long, you'll be on the other side of this crisis and better because of it.

Bottom line: if you're worried about a "what if" coming true, answer it with, "what next?" What is the next best thing you can do to prevent the "what if" from happening? Do that. Move your anxious energy into movement forward. Remember that stress (anxiety, fear) is simply the difference between what we seek to control and that which we can actually control. The choice rests between controlling more of what you can and/or letting go of the things you can't.

When you feel regret or resentment (past-focused): Commit to learning from your past experiences, decisions, and mistakes versus regretting and resenting. Once you've started the healing process, check in with yourself. See how it's going and what you're doing differently and better. Build trust with yourself that you won't shut out painful feelings, but instead you'll honor them and give yourself the time and the space you need to heal.

In both cases, it's important to celebrate the little successes. It's highly unlikely that you'll flip a switch and not travel time zones overnight. First, you'll notice yourself being more aware of which one you're in. Next, you'll notice and then pull yourself back into the present. Then, you'll notice, get present, and do the work to shed the past and take action toward your optimal future. Like you, I've had my fair share of defeat. With calm acceptance, you can see yourself as the full, glorious, torn and sewn, ripped and repaired, soiled and cleansed quilt of human pleasure and pain that you are.

~ A Pain Rebel & Trauma ~

Simply put, there are three approaches to trauma, three ways the Pain Rebel steps in, all depending upon when you can...or do...use them.

~ Pain Rebel in Prevention Mode ~

If you see a train coming ahead of time, you get off the tracks. That's the job of the "trauma guard." The **Guard** is listening and looking for potential threats and is intent on saving you misery. On any given day, we are likely saved from countless traumas due to divine intervention and the work of the Guard. It's her job to assess situations, people, and her own gut to avoid that which is likely to cause her pain. When you put on your seatbelt, thank the Guard. When you look both ways before crossing, thank the Guard. When you decline an invitation to go on a date with a person who just seems a bit "off," thank the Guard. That gut feeling you often override? Yup. That's the Guard trying to save your reckless ass. Before you jump down my literary throat, know this: Many (many, many) traumas are unavoidable because no matter how astute your Guard, someone or something else's traumatizer is working overtime and there's nothing you can do. Speaking as a person who literally got hit by a truck just riding along in a car, shit happens and there's no alert system that can save you from trauma when it's got your number. However, the more aware we are and the more we trust ourselves, the more our risk decreases. It never, ever reaches zero; it simply gives us time to catch our breath between the hits that are sure to come our way. Speaking of hits, let me introduce you to the Superhero…

~ Pain Rebel in Intervention Mode ~

Those of us who grew up watching superheroes on Saturday morning television wanted so badly to find a cape of our own. We wanted to be powerful, confident, *invincible*. Whether we saw ourselves punching and kicking our way out of danger or thinking our way through it, we craved victory's sweet nectar. We wanted a title: **Superhero**. In real life, when trauma is headed our way, our limbic system takes over and we choose fight, flight, or freeze. In the fight, we claim our superpower, choosing to intervene before trauma takes its toll. Intervention can work to reduce trauma by stopping in midstream an assault of any kind (verbal, physical), by confrontation or escape. Sometimes this superhero strategy works, when the situation is escapable and/or the person or condition is conquerable. Sometimes, the attack is just too sudden or severe to do a damn thing to stop or lessen it. In that case, we turn to the next Pain Rebel in the chain…

How We Take Our POWER Back

~ Pain Rebel in Recovery Mode ~

If the hit came too fast or hard for the Guard to avoid or the Superhero to stop, the strongest one of the team takes over: The **Healer**. The Healer knows that there is nothing we can't rise up from. That we regenerate, we recover, we rise. The Healer is the mightiest of all the Pain Rebels because she does the hardest work of all: She helps us shed that which attached itself to us, that which tricked us into believing that the trauma IS us. That's no easy task, but the Healer isn't intimidated. The Healer knows that you were made for something far greater than suffering. The Healer is well-versed in the delicate dance of how much to fight and how much to surrender along the road to recovery.

All three roles (Guard, Superhero, and Healer) hold a piece of the puzzle. Poignantly, they drive home the notion that we are worthy of protection *and* healing.

~ Protecting Ourselves ~

Years ago, I met a young woman who was struggling *hard*.

A competitive athlete, she loved her sport and perhaps even more so, her teammates. The gymnast had battled anxiety from a young age but had found ways to settle herself, usually by connecting with others and always doing her best. Her role was cheerleader...and not the kind who enjoys the limelight. She was the rare kind who did it for the love of her friends. She truly wanted to see them do their very best and was there with a supportive word, hug, or pearl of wisdom. She was kind and generous and pure of heart.

Enter: Her new coach.

This coach was hard and stern and rough around the edges, like cut glass. He was openly and repeatedly mean to the young gymnast, ridiculing her in front of her teammates. He criticized her on every event, questioning not only her talent but her effort. It became a mountain climb just to get the young woman to attend her favorite sport. She cried at the gym often and broke down in tears after every practice. Riddled with anxiety, gymnastics became the one thing in her life she wanted to get as far away from as possible. What had once been a space of calm, joy, and connection transformed into a hotbed of humiliation, fear, and exclusion. Love became hate. Peace became fear. All because of one person's misguided actions to berate the best out of his charges.

We've all been there, haven't we?

We've been run over by someone we experience as mean and harsh. Someone who we've offered free admission into our heads, letting them hijack our mental health. They become the focus of our angst and misery, the one we blame for how shitty we feel. They may not have said anything to us for days (or months or years), but they punish us with their words – the ones that play over and over again in our heads. We are diminished by someone who was sufficiently mean to injure us. We become bystanders…victims…in our own life. And the mean person gets the final – and loudest – word.

Wait…WHAT?

HELL no!

That is NOT the path of a Pain Rebel. Pain Rebels don't succumb to the brokenness of others. We don't allow their injuries to devastate us. Sure, we feel the sting of their dis-ease, but we don't hand over our power to someone else. Our power is OUR power.

But we give it away all the time. Every single time we let the wrath of others define our mood or influence our actions, we allow our power to be sapped and delivered straight to a person who is *least* entitled to it.

How We Take Our POWER Back

Imagine for a moment that you have the cutest puppy in the whole, wide world snuggled in your arms. This puppy inherently trusts you to care for it, to keep it safe and feeling loved. Unless you're a sick and twisted individual, you'd do everything possible to protect your puppy from harm.

Now, picture a mean, angry, and off-balanced person approaches you and your puppy and demands that you hand it over to them. Would you?

Of COURSE NOT! I don't even know you but I'm sure you wouldn't behave like such a careless idiot.

Yet, you do. I do. We ALL do.

How? Why?

Because that puppy represents our peace of mind, our joy, our POWER, and we hand it over all the damn time to people who are hell-bent on getting us to feel small.

We hand over our puppy. We relinquish our power. We let them win.

Repeat some powerful profanity after me: FUCK THAT.

Stop it. Stop it right now. Stop it always and forever starting today. If you get caught off guard, perhaps in a moment of delirium or mental weakness, imagine yourself retrieving that adorable bundle of fur from them and snuggling it close again. Promise to do whatever you have to do to hold dysfunctional and hurtful people away from your furry friend. Commit to protecting it against all odds because it's THAT important, THAT special.

The same goes for your power.

Don't devote your strength and power to what you seek freedom from. If you think someone is a jerk, why on earth would you let their vile words become part of your psyche? When you hand over your power, when you fail to protect yourself, you lose the opportunity to be your best self. The world loses out on getting the optimal version of you. And, equally reprehensible, the broken people collect more power, multiplying the breadth and depth of their darkness.

In true puppy power fashion, this young gymnast stepped away from the fight, knowing that the only way to hold her power and her peace was to remove herself from a toxic situation. She channeled her love for being on a team to working with younger gymnasts, providing them with the compassion and support she wished for. She reached back through the door she walked through to build other girls' strength so they could face down challenges that surely await them.

That's what Pain Rebels do. We use our burns to deepen our compassion for others traveling a similar journey. For the past couple of years, I've volunteered my time at a residential treatment program for young women who have been sex trafficked, abused, and involved in the juvenile justice and foster care system. Following one of my trainings, the teaching staff instituted a "puppy power" program to remind these girls that they did, in fact, have power. The power to live and love differently than those who had been entrusted with their care. Don't we all deserve that fresh start?

~ It Is What It Is ~

Pain either leads to more pain (to self and others) or to healing. It's like you're wandering through the woods and you come to a clearing. As you make your way onto the dusty gravel road, you see a fork in the road. One way is more of the same, the way you've been living. To the left, uncharted territory. It's brighter somehow, even though you can't see more than 20 feet away before it twists out of sight. What are you thinking? How do you feel? What do you do?

Now, imagine it's a cold morning. Because you've been working on awareness, you notice that it's really quite cold. The more you focus on it, the more it intensifies. You start to shiver. You're immediately transported to an ugly, angry, irritable place. Why didn't you bring a heavier jacket? Why do you have to live in this godforsaken state? If you'd never moved here with your ex you could be enjoying a warm, comfortable walk down the beach instead of trudging through the cold. The more you walk, the colder and more miserable you get.

Although the details of *my* inner script were different, I found myself in that same sort of dialogue while walking my dog one chilly, dark morning. When I say "chilly," I mean that the wind gusts literally hurt my face. Knowing what I know about suffering and healing, I turned inward to see if I could manifest a shift. I acknowledged the temperature. I reassured myself that it was objectively cold, but I could choose my response to it.

Inside this awareness, I detached from the shiver that had set in through shallow breaths and focused thoughts, not thoughts about the cold. *Anything* but the cold. I knew that the more I attended to the cold, the colder I felt. Focusing elsewhere didn't change the air temperature, just my mental temperature. It was what it was; giving up the fight allowed me to have an entirely different (and more pleasurable) experience.

Events themselves don't hurt us, it's how we perceive and narrate them that causes us pain. If our car got hit in a parking lot and it was our pride and joy, we might feel anger or sorrow. If we were paying for it and didn't know where the next payment was coming from, and it getting hit meant we could reap the insurance money, we might feel joy and relief. It's the meaning we place on things and our attachment to them going our way is what causes us pain.

We've all had our share of pain from attachment, and I'm no exception.

Pain Rebel

Some years ago, I was in a tightknit friendship group, a situation I'd avoided since high school. I had lots of friends but very few knew each other well or at all. But this group evolved over time and I relished being part of a "family," as scary as that idea was to me. Suffice it to say that we had very different ideas about parenting, partnering, and friendship. They focused on control and dominance whereas I focused on connection and acceptance.

Dysfunction was abound, but I was avoiding reckoning with that because of the fallout I was sure to face. I know I'm not shocking you when I tell you that the fallout happened despite my avoidance. That's what happens, right? We put duct tape to plug up a hole in the boat, but it still sinks slowly but surely. Well, this was more like the Titanic and I was Jack. I'll spare you the details about my "Rose" …

After it all blew up, I centered my thinking around them: What they might say, see, think. I hated them but was obsessed with them and their judgments of me. The very people who had hurt me (and my children by shutting them out, too) I was seeking to please…and simultaneously, punish.

They were long gone but I stayed irrevocably tied to them.

We do that. We anchor ourselves in a story that's over, continuing a connection that has long since fallen away, carrying on a relationship in our minds, our hearts…polluting both. We manifest a pain story, blocking other beautiful stories from taking hold. We clench our fists around the very thing that's burning us yet curse the wound.

~ Exercise ~

Notice yourself as you make your way through the world clenching your fist. It's a wonder how many of us do this routinely, even without direct triggers in the environment. Every time you observe yourself doing it, simply flatten your hand. Use that moment to take a few deep, relaxing, centering breaths. Feel the freedom of that simple shift spread through your body. Embrace the energy shift from tension to relaxation. You can only grab onto the next, right option when your hands are free. Speaking of freedom...

~ Surrender ~

When we run from pain, it follows us. It shows up everywhere, beckoning us to get lost in it; it's the veil that shrouds the light. The more we run, the more exhausted we get.

Or we stay and fight it, but it grows stronger with every punch. Pain is created in the struggle against it, the very definition of the word, "suffering." It lives, and thrives, in the resistance. *Resisting* creates exhaustion and misery. *Allowing* manifests authenticity and healing. We have to remind ourselves that:

"This won't kill me. This will pain me. There is a difference."

Which leads us to the gift of surrender...

Surrender is so misunderstood. It's not inaction. It's not about being passive in your life. It's not about giving up. It's *not* the opposite of a power position. Turns out, it's the first step in reclaiming more power in your life than you've ever known.

Surrender represents the balance between holding on and letting go, between driving forward and gliding along.

Surrender is a powerful tool because you are concentrating your power where it is influential: In the thoughts you can hold, the feelings you can indulge, the actions you can take. You aren't trying to control everyone else's role, and in doing so, you let go of your attachment to the outcome. You consider which fight you want to fight. You hold fast to your strength to respond to whatever happens, knowing that you'll figure it out. Like a martial arts champion, your power exists in not in controlling the fight in advance, or getting lost in regrets over prior matches, but in training and conditioning so when a hit comes, you're ready.

How do you surrender?

Surrender to the **outcome**. Take action in the **process**.

Take the example of a job hunter. Countless times I've coached people out of trying to manage both the interviewer's perceptions and their own presentation. Do me a favor: Give up on the former and focus on the latter. You can't control what they think of you. You can only control how you show up. Sure, one influences the other, but you cannot control both sides of the equation. That's a misuse of your energy. And your energy is everything.

~ Mantra Exercise ~

Surrender is arduous, especially when pain comes knocking at your door, whether it's past or present. We struggle to accept pain on its own terms. This life-changing mantra has saved my sanity more than once.

I allow the pain:

~ To come
~ To teach
~ To awaken
~ To go

Notice the shift in your awareness, and energy, as you let this chant wash over you. Feel the acceptance of the present moment fill you will resolve to be stronger and more resilient going forward.

How We Take Our POWER Back

~ Of Course ~

If you read my third book, **Stuck U.**, you know that the critical part of acceptance is accepting that you got to where you are in the present as a natural result of what you believed and did in the past. Nevertheless, we spend much too much time blaming ourselves for being where we are. We ruminate over all the mistakes we've made. We self-flagellate over and over again, trying to internally punish our way out of it. This is time we can't reclaim, and it doesn't do a damn thing.

Hear me when I say this: Of course you held onto the lessons you held onto. Of course you found yourself here, in this moment, carrying the baggage you're carrying. Of course you've developed the coping mechanisms you did. Of course you employed the tactics you employed. Tactics? Tactics are behavioral approaches you use to get your needs met. It's the way we survive. Which tactics we use are defined by the belief structures we adopted about what our possible choices were for getting our needs met and ensuring our survival. We had limited choices because we had limiting belief structures. Feeling distraught about that? Feeling the feelings of loss, regret, and anger? Do this:

~ True Voice Exercise ~

Take a seat in a quiet, comfortable place. centering in on the feelings that occupy your chest and abdomen. Close your eyes and take 3 cleansing breaths in and out. Place one hand gently on your heart while placing the other softly on your belly. Bring to mind a picture of yourself at a time when you were strong, certain, and full of love…before the world took away your footing. Ask him/her to guide you back to your essence. Ask for their strength, their clarity, and their love. Express compassion for yourself. Know that you got here so you can get to another place. This is temporary.

Pain Rebel

If there is no vision of you with those qualities because damage was inflicted upon you at an early age, try this adaptation:

Imagine a friend or family member who embodies those characteristics. Ask them to sit with you. Ask them to place their hands on your hands and share their essence with you. Feel their strength, clarity, and love fill you. For me, it's my grandma and I visit with her often. She believes in me when I forget to believe in myself. I hope you have someone like that to fill you. If you don't, please borrow my grandma: She's got enough to share.

To close out this discussion, I'll leave you with this surrender quote I crafted that is posted on my bathroom mirror. It helps me to practice active "emptying."

I am open to the space

I allow for growth and enlightenment

Space is where growth occurs

Wisdom emerges in the darkness

Quiet allows for inspiration

Key Chapter Concepts

- Healing mechanisms are better than coping mechanisms.
- Moving forward requires that we assess the past and the now.
- Pain Rebels exist in prevention, intervention, and healing mode.
- Accepting, and surrendering to, the moment as it is holds immense power.
- You are where you are because of where you've been and how you've thought about it.

---

*"Oh what we could be if we stopped carrying
the remains of who we were." ~ Tyler Knott Gregson*

7

IT'S TERMINAL

"We're all just walking each other home." ~ Ram Dass

~ Life's Final Mystery ~

Way to bring the sunshine, Dr. B! Kick off an entire chapter talking about *death*.

The truth is that the only way to embrace *life* is to confront *death*.

To passionately live your life, you must be acutely tuned into the imminent nature of its guaranteed end. We are mortal. No one is getting out of this alive, as the saying goes. In the interim, we will all suffer great losses and formidable wins. We will lose every last person and experience we get attached to by death, divorce, or discord. We may leave first, or we may be left. But there will be a leaving.

We get this one life to live and we need to **live** it. Notice that I didn't say, "suffer through it," though that's what we can get roped into if we don't commit to something better. Pain Rebels see that hollow, burdened existence and insist on a different course. Pain Rebels want a life full and *un*burdened. Pain Rebels know how hard life can be but insist on not making it any harder than it needs to be. It's short; by many accounts, way *too* short. When we reach the end of our journey, we certainly won't be wishing we held onto *more* hurts, been saddled with *heavier* misery. I'll bet we only regret the time and energy we wasted on being stuck and miserable when we could have been free and joyful. As we've reviewed, we are certain to encounter pain along the way; what we do with that pain is what defines the course and content of our remaining time on the planet. Truth be told:

Life is a beautiful, terrifying, wanderlust adventure. Embrace it all. Find your guides and your companions and LIVE.

As I approach the big 5-0, I'm struck by all the stories of early deaths. What do we do when confronted by the impending cloak of death? Well, we assert the illusion of control by enrolling in yoga classes, eating green, and taking the stairs. But what about our spirits? How do we purify our mental health? What's the kale for THAT?

Pain rebelling.

Pain Rebels play the long game, with one eye on their final destination in order to give value to the path that brings them there.

~ Backward Planning ~

Military members tout the importance of backward planning to ensure a successful operation. In its simplest terms, backward planning means starting with a clear understanding of where you want to end up and figuring out what steps are essential to get you there.

Life works that way, too.

How We Take Our POWER Back

During my time on this planet, I've seen the vast majority of people motivated by a goal or two, often placed there by external expectations. Maybe their parents told them that being rich was the morally superior position, so they've been on a quest to amass wealth. Perhaps society told them that being beautiful and popular was the road to happiness, so they're consumed by fitness and social acceptance.

There's nothing wrong with the desire to be beautiful, popular, or rich. Being any or all of those things is super cool. The emerging problem is where you're focusing your efforts and why.

It's the "Someday Solution."

Someday, when I'm thin, life will be better. Someday when I find the partner of my dreams, my happy life can begin. Someday, when I've "made it" career-wise, I'll enjoy my life.

There's no such thing as someday. Someday is for suckers. It's a bullshit story sold to the part of our subconscious actively suppressing our fear of death, keeping us from being happy.

When you're saddled with pain, suffice it to say that you're not happy. In the last couple of decades, we've learned a lot about happiness. The happiness literature (yes, there's such a thing) tells us that we don't find happiness – at least not for more than a fleeting moment – after we get to "someday." Why? For several reasons. One, our satiation point moves forward with our goal attainment. We reach one goal and we immediately set another, spending no time at all being satisfied with where we are. Two, our definitions are obscure.

Take wealth, for instance. When I was fifteen, having a ton of money meant very different things than it did when I was thirty. Most of us spend what we make (and then some), so the needle is persistently in flux away from where we are. There's always "richer." Same goes for pretty. I'm in my late forties now and I can tell you that I wish I was as attractive/thin/wrinkle-free as I was in my early twenties. If you'd asked me then if I was happy with my looks, I'd have scoffed at you. When we count on a particular goal (or some series of them) to deliver happiness, we don't experience it, at least not for very long.

What's the alternative?

Like any good attorney, I never ask a question I don't know the answer to.

Start with the end in mind.

Instead of picking a point or points along the journey that need to look a certain way, envision how you'd evaluate your life in retrospect. Putting yourself at Heaven's gate, meeting St. Peter for those of Christian faith, is a good place to start.

I taught Catholic education to first and second graders when my daughters were enrolled in the classes, which was comical given that I was a divorced, single mom who'd been baptized just shy of my thirtieth birthday. But, hey, I can think of bigger errors in judgment…

I digress.

So, there I was, somewhat in charge of the religious formation of close to a dozen youngsters. Inspired and invested, I answered each of their innocent yet precocious questions as honestly, intelligently, and simply as I could. One evening, a little boy approached me and asked, "what's Heaven like?"

Nothing like a question as complex as time itself to stump me in front of a group of eager inquisitors.

Unintimidated, I delivered the following response:

"When you get to the pearly gates, you're asked three questions before they will allow you to enter. First, did you have FUN? Second, did you use the gifts and talents I gave you to the best of your ability?

Third, did you do your best to leave every situation and person better than you found them? If your answers were 'yes,' the response will be, 'come on in!' Oh, and there's a whole bunch of chocolate and puppies!"

You might not personally believe in the concept of a heaven, and that's cool. However, if your moral compass is guiding you, it most likely has some version of "live a life of worth and value" embedded in it. The question then becomes, how do YOU define that life? What will your life look like in aggregate? Will you care about the number of promotions you received if they have no meaning beyond external validation? Or will you value you them because they increased your influence with people and causes you love?

There's a much tougher question to wrestle with: What if you die before you reach one of your goalposts (money, fame, fortune, marriage, beauty)?

Unfortunately, many of us do. Despite our best attempts to negotiate with Death, we aren't in charge. We can influence our path toward our eventual demise, but we can't make it agree with our plans. We often die before we are ready. We face our maker before we are "done." We leave with to-do lists, bills to pay, events to attend, and projects to complete. Worse than any of those practicalities, we leave with words unspoken, good deeds undone, and love unexpressed.

Pain Rebels do it differently.

Pain Rebels see the end coming early on. We know we have an unknown expiration date, so we start with the end in mind. We know our lives are meaningful only when we refuse to get lost in the mundane and distracting minutia of life. We walk with death each and every day. Death's certainty is our beloved companion, reminding us to live and love with fervent intention. Life reminds us of its fragility every day: All-too-frequent news of loved ones burdened with illness and injury, tragedies the world over, and our own daily decay.

Pain Rebel

When the world delivers a crushing blow to a Pain Rebel, our instinct is to view it in the context of our short life. We know life will end without our permission so to avoid that realization is a waste of an already short existence. We confront our mortality with acceptance...and love. We know that the more we embrace it with affection, the more it improves our lives. We refuse to forget how little time we really have, so we vow to make life's span meaningful.

Meaning is made on our journey by returning to those questions I posed to my young students:

Did you have fun?

Did you use your gifts to best of your abilities?

Did you do your best to leave each situation better than you found it?

If you have the luxury of hitting the pause button at the precise moment of your death, how are you apt to answer those questions? Will each be a resounding "yes" or will you hesitate, hung up on procrastinated plans and rationalizing away the things you always meant to do and be? Pain Rebels are the lead players in their own lives, dismissing the incessant distractions and mind games we create to deny death's reality; the very things that encourage us to live life passively and unintentionally.

Pain Rebels live with clear intention.

Intentions are the foundation under the goal, the deeper reason for the goal. When I set an intention, I'm putting the full force of my attention to stay the course because I have a fire in my belly to reach the goal because the goal is consistent with my values. Goals without values are hollow. Set goals anchored in your life purpose or skip them altogether. What is your life's purpose? It's really simple to uncover when you get right down to it. It's what you value about your tour here on earth. Pain Rebels zero-in on their core values and leverage them to live a life of purpose and intention.

What does an intention (versus a goal) sound like? My intention for writing this book was to stir people into a deeper awareness so that they could reclaim their power and live with less pain. My intention comes from love, compassion, and passion, anchored in *desire*. My goal was to finish the book at a certain time and sell a certain number of copies. My goal is more grounded in checks and balances, anchored in *results*. Both serve us, but goals without intentions are meaningless and wholly unsatisfying, whereas intentions without goals can free us to simply celebrate our innate gifts and generosity of spirit, regardless of the outcome.

~ The Dash ~

What does looking back on a life well-lived mean to you? Where does all this pain fit in? Do you have room for it in the narrative of a life well spent?

I've read so many obituaries and eulogies over the years, attended my fair share of funerals, and given an unsettling number of eulogies.

I've even seen my own funeral a hundred times.

No, I'm not a time-traveler. One of the ways I dealt with pain when I was younger was to flirt with death. By sixteen, I'd amassed three suicide attempts, the last one landing me in intensive care. I drank myself unconscious on several occasions in high school, not to mention all the times I rode in cars with inebriated drivers. Two years into college, I pulled my car in front of oncoming traffic and, without the aid of a secured seatbelt, rammed my head through my car's windshield…twice.

My sorrow was deep but my desire for recognition, for connection, ran deeper. I wanted to be seen, loved, and appreciated. I wanted to hear all the things people say about loved ones at their funeral said about me. So, I fantasized about my own funeral. I imagined what others would say about me, how much those who hurt me would regret their actions. The only problem was I could never enjoy that experience because I'd have to be dead for it to be true.

Then my daydream slightly shifted to being close to death, comatose, able to hear and sense others but unresponsive. Spending time in this alternate reality presented me with the poignant gift of seeing how I wished to be remembered; how I hoped I'd have affected others; and all the things I'd make sure I said to those I loved…and even those I held in contempt…for I knew those fantasies of a second chance at death's door were wanderlust.

These musings started me on a path to settle up my priorities and live with them clear in mind. We've all heard that our priorities change when we are told of our impending demise. When we get that diagnosis that will cut our life off earlier than we'd hoped, we laugh louder, work less (unless it's work we're passionate about), and love more freely. When I saw the headlights of that oncoming car in August of 2018, I begged for more time. More time with my daughters, more time to give more of myself to the world. More time in the space between my birth year and my death year, the dash that'll mark my years on this planet. That's the dash that encompasses everything.

~ Exercise ~

Pain Rebels know what they value by crafting their own eulogy, the final narrative of their life. Want to be a Pain Rebel? Write your own eulogy. What does a well-lived life mean to you? Where does pain fit in? How do you want to be seen at the end? Knowing that, you'll start living today like you mean it.

How We Take Our POWER Back

~ Good News Network ~

The good news about anchoring ourselves with the end in mind is that we are incentivized to take deliberate steps to change our actions if we're headed in the wrong direction. The even *better* news is that every time you learn something or do something differently you change your brain. That's right. You actually change the way your brain organizes and processes information due to a cool thing called "neuroplasticity." There's new research coming out all the time that points to the amazing power of our brains to change over time, even if we are old. We have brain plasticity. Our brains change in two main ways: Structurally and functionally. Structural changes refer to the ways a brain's physical structure is changed through learning. Functional changes refer to how a brain relocates functions from a damaged to an undamaged area.

The best driver of any of these changes is your behavior. Want to know the most fantastic news? When you struggle, your brain experiences more learning and realizes more structural change. Bottom line: we can heal and change at a core level. Change is not only possible, it's guaranteed. All it takes is a commitment to it. A commitment to what you value so you can change in the right direction. Ready to examine those values?

~ What Are YOUR Priorities? ~

One of my favorite sayings is:

Don't **ask** someone what they value. Instead, **watch** how they spend their time and their money.

What would your values look like? Do you say you value family and health but spend most of your time isolated at work and eating at the drive-thru? Do you say you value charitable causes but never volunteer or donate money?

94

Pain Rebel

How will YOU define a life well-spent? What's REALLY important to you?

I do strategic planning retreats for organizations large and small, helping teams and divisions get crystal clear on their mission. What are they good at? What does the world/their customer need? How do they leverage their unique offerings and gifts to meet what the market wants (or vice versa)?

The same logic applies to our lives. What are YOUR gifts? How can you hone them to best share them with the world? What gives your life meaning? When I'm working with individual clients, we do strategic life planning. I challenge my clients to come up with three words that define their purpose in life so that they can plan it strategically. We drive toward power words like:

Inspire
Guide
Lead
Share
Enjoy
Connect
Entertain
Protect
Help
Defend

Curious about what my three are? Guide, Inspire, and Connect. When I'm not doing any (or all) of these three, I feel depleted. I know that I'm not living to my fullest potential. I'm not leaving the best of me in the world, so I feel unfulfilled.

How could your "power words" help you?

These words anchor you to an "end in mind" philosophy. You live not just WITH purpose but IN purpose. In the seconds' or days' notice you have for your certain end, you won't question if your time here was meaningful. You'll KNOW. The moment of death's arrival may be a mystery, but your purposeful life won't be.

Life is what happens before we say goodbye. Like I told you earlier, we will say goodbye to everyone we ever meet. Ever love. Who we build our lives with. It's just a matter of when, where, and how. Will we go and leave them behind, or will they leave us one by one? This truth brings us great sorrow AND massive joy, if we pay attention. In knowing that we are finite, we can embrace the chance to live this life large, out loud, and with minimal regrets.

That's what Pain Rebels do.

First, let me ask you:

How is your relationship to and experience of pain standing in the way of you fully experiencing the life you envision? Your one, best, phenomenal life?

~ Don't Let Stupid Shit Fuck with Your One & Only Life ~

Was the title a little harsh? Perhaps. You know what's harsher? Letting you stew in your own angry, sad, disappointed, hurt, resentful juices one minute longer before smacking you awake so you don't waste one more moment of your *very* temporary existence. They call me a cage rattler for good reason: I'm banging on the bars trying to jolt you out of your stupor, the one that most everyone you know is trapped in.

In our modern world we are lulled into complacency. Sure, many of us have goals. Legions of us are striving toward one thing or another. But the one thing we are forgetting in all of this nonsense? Who the fuck we are, what we stand for, and what difference we will make before we depart this one, all-too-short life. I've met far too many people who woke up right before they died. Who figured out how senseless so many concerns they'd been obsessed with really were.

Their fat thighs.

Their thin bank accounts.

Their brown lawn.

Their small house.

Their big problems.

Nothing mattered as they reached the end except the very things they'd shoved into the corners of their minds to get through each day:

Love.

Legacy.

Fun.

To live a life of light. Light in darkness. Light in worry. Light in resentment. Light in cares.

But right now maybe you feel like an unevolved Goldilocks; nothing fits so *everything* feels uncomfortable.

Are you waiting for a gold-embossed invitation to take part in your own life? Do you think your fairy godmother will arrive any minute now with your gown and chariot?

Well, here it is and here I am.

Let's GO.

"In any given moment we have two options: To step forward into growth or step back into safety." ~ Abraham Maslow

8

CLEAN SLATE

"Put the pen down someone else gave you. No one ever drafted a life worth living on borrowed ink." ~ Jack Kerouac

Imagine you've waited all year to see your favorite band in concert. You scraped and you saved to reserve enough money for front row tickets. You'll be able to see the whites of their eyes, and droplets of their sweat might reach you. Racing to grab tickets before they undoubtedly sold out, you've counted the days till you could reap the reward of your efforts. The opening act departed the stage; now it's time for the main attraction. Convinced this experience will change your life, you cannot contain your excitement.

This page right here, this is your front-row seat to your emotional freedom and unadulterated joy. They've been eagerly waiting for you...

~ The Big Reveal ~

Anyone who has ever heard me speak walks away with one prevailing mantra stuck in their head: Power comes from choice. So how do you tap into your capacity for choice? Awareness. When you hone your awareness of the world in and around you, you expand your consciousness of choice, seeing how each moment offers you a chance to choose your thoughts, feelings, and behaviors.

Awareness equals choice and choice equals power.

It's time to mobilize your awareness to spur your curiosity. Start pondering why you're so tired, overwhelmed, sensitive, volatile, and maybe even hopeless. There are answers and paths out of your old patterns.

Now that we are experts on pain and have let go of the nonsense we believed about it, we need to revisit two things:

1. Pain is deepened by the meaning we make of it. You need to be willing to challenge the stories you've been telling yourself about pain and its place in your life.
2. Hurt people hurt people, so if you want less pain to come to you, you must commit to not recycling it to others.

Sound like a tall order to fill? It's challenging but completely doable, believe me. One thing I do know for sure: The more you approach anything with curiosity the more prepared you will be to change it. This next section is chock full of ways for you to do just that: Change your stories, self-talk, and, well, **LIFE**.

The prevailing storyline goes like this…We are caught in a bind of believing limiting (sometimes, terrible) things about ourselves due to early experiences, often our very earliest. Originally, we were on a direct path to joy and abundance. Unfortunately, it got interrupted. Compounding the problem, we go on to operate from the interruption. We forgot our destiny.

How can we remember it?

At the end of the last chapter, I inquired about how your relationship to and experience of pain was standing in your way of living your best life. I was challenging your awareness so you could see the choices available to you to change your life. Well, with no further delay, let's get to it.

~ *The Price of Being Right* ~

Awareness invites some level of understanding, so let's take this beast apart piece by piece.

We are in control of only three things in this lifetime: Our thoughts, feelings, and behaviors. I call this my "TFB model." When presenting my TFB model to audiences, I get the most pushback for the "feelings" component. Many people can't buy that they have responsibility for their feelings (and sometimes the same holds true for their thoughts). We accept that we are responsible for our behavior more often than not, unless someone "makes" us feel a certain way and we believe that there's only one legitimate response.

Ours.

Our brains are thought, feeling, and behavior machines. When a thought crosses our minds, it creates a biochemical reaction that leads to a feeling consistent with the thought. Then, more thoughts follow to support the feeling we're having. For example, you see a spider. You identify yourself as a person who is afraid of spiders so that thought spurs the biochemical surge that leads you to feeling terror. From that feeling, you indulge thoughts about the spider's creepy-crawly nature, bites, and creepy eyes. Your terror intensifies. You run screaming from the room.

Was there another way?

Certainly.

We have built a life around our interpretations and judgments. When crisis or stress hits, we feel like passengers on a runaway train.

The way we see things, the world, is fixed. We believe things to be exactly as we see them, but how we see them hurts and limits us. We hold fast to our worldview, convinced that our way is the only way. So, we think, feel, and act on it.

But far too often, we are on the wrong track to claim our abundant birthright. Our current track is built on poorly informed and misleading ideas, agreed upon when we had no other reasonable option to consider. When we were young, often powerless, and unable to even see that we had a choice to *make*.

The ways we've associated with events, people, and ourselves keep us bound to early pain, and we inevitably seek more of the familiar.

We want to return home. Even if home poisons us.

We cling to our narrative. We are fiercely loyal to it and will keep it going perpetually, even in the face of great hardship. Whenever my kids struggled with anything from a tough homework assignment to a sports skill, I was the (annoying) mom who would respond to their "I can't" with "you're right." If we say "I can't" then we will move (or not move) Heaven and Earth to keep that narrative as truth.

Being right eclipses being happy.

Considerable pain comes from agreeing with the negative voices that entered into our insides from the outside. By believing them and carrying them forward through life, we beat ourselves and others up with them.

This is the pain in our contracts.

Why do I call them "contracts?"

I call them "contracts" because they include terms, conditions, and agreements, just like written contracts. We all live under a social contract, the infrastructure that holds together our society. In the

United States, our social contract supports the American Dream. It promises life, liberty, and the pursuit of happiness. Our capitalist contract promises that if we work hard, we will get ahead; if we follow the rules, we will live peacefully. Unfortunately, we know all too well that it's more complicated than that...

At a personal level, we also have contracts. And, just like our social contract, most of us didn't sign our contracts consciously because we were born into and raised within them.

Everyone has contracts. These contracts act like an operating system does on your computer: You can't see it, but everything you do depends on it and is filtered through it. Collectively, your contracts are basically your "dynamic" or narrative. They tell you how the world works and how you work within it. You follow them because you feel obligated, believing that they are how things *must* be. They create an expected response. If this, then that. You know what to expect and how to respond because you have a set of rules that direct you. They keep you safe (through predictability) and in line. You rarely question their validity, unless or until it's pointed out that they aren't working for you. Even then, you might be unhappy but it's a familiar unhappiness. You seek pain because it's comfortable and known.

Contracts tell us what we agree to believe (and thereby feel about and act) about events, situations, people, or things. Our contracts refer to:

~ Why things happened the way that they did
~ What our role was in it
~ What roles others played
~ What we expect will happen in the future.

Since we've "agreed" to them by being in certain relationships and situations, they're contracts. Seeing it as a contract versus as an elusive dynamic gives us the power and responsibility to examine and amend it. We form contracts far before we have the capacity to do so, contracts that set up our mental models about what we can expect from the world, others, and ourselves. We stay beholden to them, far beyond their useful shelf life. That's how pain gets passed from generation to generation. Our early experiences shape our contracts and our contracts define our lives. It's a twisted game of "hot potato" where everyone gets burned.

Contracts are efficient, much in the same way prejudices are. They provide safe shortcuts that don't challenge our worldview. And, similarly, they keep us stuck and injured, limited by something that we *can* change. If we've been hurt, holding a contract that people can't be trusted allows us to stay safely protected from them. Can you see how that serves us?

Common things, traits, and definitions that we form contracts about include: Love, connection, power, kindness, peace, anger, fear, success, virtue, loyalty, sex, passion, meaning of life, control. Our contracts may say things like:

~ Love means pain, suffering, and playing the martyr.
~ Power is evil.
~ Money is bad (or conversely, *everything*).
~ Attractiveness equals worth.
~ Control over people/outcomes is necessary and desirable.
~ Perfection is the only way to thrive (or survive).
~ Fear is weakness, evil, and the enemy.
~ Loyalty (at all costs, to all ends) is virtuous and is required for love.
~ Success equals money, power, and workaholism.
~ Power is the only way to feel/stay safe.
~ Being sexy is how you establish your worth.

Contracts are something we take on as "truth" and follow with patterns of thought, feeling, and action that reinforce it as such. If our contract about love is that it's supposed to hurt, and our partner *isn't* causing us discomfort, we will likely leave or create a conflict to bring pain to ourselves.

If we have unhealthy contracts,
we form unhealthy attachments.

Nothing is as frightening as waking up to your life and coming face-to-face with your contracts, knowing that they're responsible for the level of pain and disruption in your life all along. I hope you'll proceed with self-compassion, knowing that:

You only knew what you knew so you could only do what you did.

Who do we make these contracts with?

~ Our family of origin, where most contracts originate from, paving the way for future ones
~ Nuclear family
~ Significant other
~ Friendship circle
~ Professional identity/work family
~ Personal identity/self-concept (including political identity)
~ Faith/spiritual identity/higher power.

Each definition, each contract, is a choice. We choose how we define these things, despite the fact that other definitions are always possible. Becoming aware of these definitions as choices…choices made and reinforced through contracts…empowers us to make new ones and change them as we go. Our thinking becomes more flexible. Flexibility equals growth…and power.

In turn, we can adapt to a new level of awareness: We know that nothing is definite or permanent. Even and especially our relationships with others.

Pain Rebel

"Let go of what you're used to.
Wait for what you deserve." ~ R.H. Sin

Boy, you could reduce the number of boyfriends I had by three-quarters if I'd just listened to *that* sage advice!

Did you know that you have a relationship contract with everyone in your life?

What? You don't remember signing it?

You did. You agreed to a set of expectations that each of you could have about each other. Expectations that may or may not have been discussed, but that each of you hold about the other person.

Maybe it's that they will always tell you the truth, no matter how hurtful. Maybe it's that you will always keep things light and cheerful, staying away from anything deep and meaningful. People sign these contracts every day when they enter into relationships and set up their "dance," their relationship dynamic. Figuring out what those contracts are is worth investigating. Why?

Ahh, so many reasons. First off, I'm a huge proponent of awareness. If you are aware of something, you can make deliberate actions versus just going along for the ride. Second, when you see your relationships as based on these contracts, you can see how certain agreements might not be serving you. You can appreciate that it's not necessarily about who the other person is or who you are; it's about the relationship contract you both signed. Lastly, when you can see your relationship contracts clearly, you can trust the people you're in relationship with to be exactly as the contract spells out. Well, that is, unless or until they decide to change the contract.

When I was in a serious relationship years ago, I performed this very assessment. I was in a verbally and emotionally abusive relationship and was feeling increasingly miserable. The man I was involved with hadn't changed during our relationship: He had been abusive from jump. I knew who he was when I started dating him, yet I continued to be with him. I signed a relationship contract that permitted him to hurt me and for me to feel responsible for his wrath. I went along with this contract for almost a decade.

At one pivotal point, I used my training as a marriage and family therapist to see our relationship through a lens of roles we were playing and rules we were abiding by. It was through this perspective that I could see our contract, and I decided that I wanted to amend it. Transform it, really. I didn't want to be "that girl" anymore. I was changing, opening up my own pipeline of awesome and this contract wasn't a fit for who I was becoming.

So, I told him I wanted to change our contract and we did, and we lived happily ever after. The end.

Yeah, not so much.

I *did* tell him I wanted to change our contract (and I put it in language like that). He didn't care. He was comfortable in our contract and saw no need to change it. He saw me as violating the contract because he didn't think that contracts could or should be changed.

Ever.

What good did it do for me to know about all this contract stuff if he wasn't going to change?

It did all the good that ever really mattered. It was central to me getting clear and staying as peaceful as I could as I let go of the relationship. I knew that I had signed the contract, too, so I had allowed his behavior all along. I was not responsible for his abusive treatment of me, mind you. But I was able to accept his anger at me for wanting to change the contract because he didn't sign on for *that*. *His* contract said "forever" no matter what.

Pain Rebel

It's that which we reveal in one another that terrifies us. We date the person who is angry all the time to find the part of ourselves that thinks we aren't worthy of peace. We befriend the person who is unavailable because we must find the part of ourselves that thinks we don't deserve love. The challenge is to rise up and fix that which needs to be fixed. And we will find that right in the nearest mirror.

I'm offering you this section in this very book to be your cue to assess your relationship contracts, to see if they serve you and your plan for change.

Below are some questions to ask yourself about your relationships (personal and professional) to see if your contracts might need to be updated or rewritten entirely.

What are the rules about your relationship (who is allowed/supposed to do what?)?

What have you agreed to that now feels uncomfortable or yucky?

What are the déjà vu moments where you're aggravated again (and again and again) about something that went on between you?

Are you holding requirements (boundary-based) or expectations (silent hopes)? Has someone agreed to your requirements, to be in relationship with you? Then you have an agreement. I dated an engineer who often spoke of his "requirements list" on work projects. They were clear, written, formal, and detailed elements that were necessary in order to build and complete their assignment. In our relationships (personal or professional), this "requirements list" is also known as our "boundaries." These are the invisible, but powerful, set of lines that cannot be crossed without consequence or redress. What are some of yours (yes, you'll need more paper!)?

See anything interesting? Think it might be time to renegotiate?

You have to address yesterday in order to fix today. Not by reliving it, but by healing the part you carried forward into today. You can't fix what happened yesterday by only focusing on today...you have to go back to heal what hurt way back when so that you can carry forward the healing into today...just like you did with the pain.

~ DYS-Connection ~

Humans are social creatures. Sadly, if you ask anyone what they struggle with most they'll tell you: Relationships.

I contend that the main reason is the dysfunction of our contracts. Intimacy comes with great risk and greater reward. How we see that tradeoff is anchored in our contracts. Most of us have been showing up to our most intimate relationships in *pain*, not in *love*. We come from our wounds and not from our love. It's no wonder things go off the rails. We want a partner, but we don't know how to *be* a partner.

If you're anything like me, your old contracts had you connecting with those who could not truly connect. In my case, this allowed me to feel unloved and "safe" at the same time. I kept finding more of that familiar pain. If a pleasing, easy relationship came my way, I bailed. WTF, Bridget? But it made perfect sense. I was a product of every decision and circumstance that came before. It was no surprise that I'd be clueless as to how to attract or navigate a healthy relationship. Lucky for me, I'm on a spiritual journey of growth so I've collected lots of learning!

If you're out there feeling unloved, hear this: You are loved. Welcome it in with open arms. Bathe in it. It's always there, even when you shut your eyes and your heart to it and turn your back on it. You are not alone. Love is all around you. It's all around me, too. Perhaps it doesn't show up in the form we demand.

Maybe we ordered a boyfriend or girlfriend for Christmas, and an elderly neighbor in need of companionship comes knocking? Recognize the love that just showed up! You don't have to sleep in the street just because the house you're in isn't the home you once imagined. Maybe you'll get the boy/girlfriend next year? For now, receive…and give…the love that's there. Isn't that what you want your *new contracts* to support?

Before we tackle your contracts, we need to look at one core power shift we must make so that you'll commit to the end result.

~ Breaking Painful Pacts ~

Old contracts are lies we tell ourselves about who we are and what we deserve. We've been handed some pretty hard blows by life at one time or another. We collect those as evidence, like crime scene investigators, to prove that we are undeserving of joy, love, abundance, and peace. That our lives are destined to be hard and sad. That we don't deserve any better than that.

**Just because you _DIDN'T_ hear it,
doesn't make it not true/valid/real**

Just as,

**Just because you _DID_ hear it,
doesn't make it true/valid/real**

The only thing that makes anything true/valid/real is when we assign it a particular meaning. We could choose another meaning or offer another interpretation. No one gets to do this for us. That's what rewriting our contracts is all about!

Did you deserve to hear that you're not deserving? Imagine telling your BFF that bullshit story. You wouldn't, would you? Then what makes you so special? You've made mistakes? You've failed? You've been less than perfect (gasp!)? JOIN THE CLUB. Simply put:

Old contracts: What you've _tolerated_.

New contracts: What you _deserve_.

Taking stock of our old contracts allows us to see the lies we've bought into that don't serve us. Growing up, I was locked out of the club my sister and mother belonged to: Depression. Sure, I attempted suicide on several occasions, but I didn't identify myself with my despair, so I didn't belong to their club. In my family, we connected over sorrow and desperation, suffering and hurt. Suffering was the only currency that had value. I tolerated suffering but I sure didn't deserve it.

When we acknowledge the patterns brought on by our contracts, we can decide consciously if we want to continue in the dance. We can break these painful pacts, releasing the pain they brought. We allow ourselves to see hope and entertain our true potential, and _that_ is exquisite.

If we stay stuck in our old contracts, we stay stuck in our same patterns and experiences. We *say* we want meaning in our lives, but our old contracts stand in our way. Searching for meaning in a meaningless job/relationship/existence is a recipe for disaster and depression. You don't have to quit your job/relationship (and certainly not your existence!), but if you stay, you need to shift and renegotiate your expectations. Remember, expectations are things you believe that you or others ***should*** do. Intentions are things that you ***want*** to do or create (or ask for in the form of an agreement). Expectations are riddled with guilt and shame. Intentions (and agreements) are abundant with power.

Speaking of expectations, here's a sample list of things to let go of that might help you in reshaping your contracts.

~ Expectations of how things are supposed to be
~ Relationships that hurt (vs. challenge) us
~ Fear
~ Loyalty to pain, and hurtful people
~ Self-loathing
~ Procrastination (and it's frequent twin, perfectionism)
~ Clinging to hope when it's toxic
~ Resentment, anger, judgment (toward yourself and others)
~ Beliefs and habits that derail, shrink you from your power
~ Victim mentality
~ Old stories you tell that paint you in a dark and limiting way.

And my personal favorite: That happiness is something you *strive for* not something that you *are*. In other words: Thinking that you'll never have, or be, enough.

~ Confronting Never Enough ~

Do you ever wonder when you'll have, or be, enough?

How We Take Our POWER Back

Enough money. Enough time. Enough love. Enough stuff. Enough success. Enough happiness. Enough memories. Enough space. Enough LIFE. When will our efforts produce ENOUGH?

Just a few years ago, a stellar, robust, larger-than-life woman who was like a second mother to me succumbed to cancer. I took my daughters to the memorial service and I wept for her, her husband, children, grandchildren, and every last person who loved her throughout her short life. The rabbi wove a beautiful service together, apparently like only rabbis can do. Referencing the Talmud, she spoke about the elusive concept of "enough." (Thankfully for me, she spoke in English for this segment of the service so I could grasp the powerful message she offered. I know a few choice words in Yiddish, but I doubt those would have done me much good.)

The message was simple: We will never have enough. Well, not in this lifetime, anyway. We will always want more. Even when we are happy, we will thirst for more happiness, for more time to revel in, for more people with which to share it with. At first, this struck me as deeply sad. Then, in true B- (what I call myself) fashion, I got even more thinky thinky and realized how freeing this concept is! If NOTHING is ever enough, then that means I can stop this senseless, frustrating, and downright crazy-making pursuit of it! I'll never HAVE it, so I can stop trying to GET it! Yowzers!! This brilliant and perfectly placed rabbi just saved me about 3 bazillion hours of therapy, gallons of tears, and countless bottles of wine.

Scratch that. I'll still drink plenty of wine.

Only now, I'll do it to celebrate the amount I DO have. The money. The love. The time. The stuff. The success. The joy. The memories. The LIFE. I'll rejoice in THAT, knowing that it's the only *enough* I'll ever know. How can this approach free YOU from angst and frustration? It's so darn simple and one of the most profound things I've shared.

You can now live in THIS moment. In THIS situation. In THIS experience, not yearning for what you don't yet have, but rather celebrating with wild abandon whatever it is that you DO have. The suffering we experience comes from the gaps: The difference between what we want (or expect) and what we have. Letting go of the quest for "enough" removes a massive amount of this suffering. It equalizes what we want with what we have.

Happiness isn't having what you want.... it's wanting what you have. It's being satisfied with your current state. There is joy in striving, but we should never forget to be happy *now*. Because, folks, truer than true: Now is all we have. Let go of that foolish notion of "enough"...and feel a powerful shift in your life, accepting things as they are, not as you envision them to be someday. We don't have someday. We have to-day. Eat that up, people. Eat. That. Up.

One thing that blocks us from relishing in today is that nagging...often, smothering...sensation we harbor that **we** aren't enough. No matter how much "enough" (stuff, accolades, etc.) we gather, we never feel on the *inside* what we look like on the *outside*. This "imposter syndrome" is the most common ailment of anyone I've ever coached, because we all started off innocent and impressionable. We believed broken messages, often from broken people. In turn, we signed old contracts that have us believing nonsense about what our worth is...and is based on.

Ready to let that shit go?

Key Chapter Concepts

- Awareness equals choice and choice equals power.
- We are only in control of our thoughts, feelings, and actions.
- Our contracts tell us what we agree to believe about situations, people, or things. Old contracts represent what we allowed. Our new contracts affirm what we deserve.

"My best teachers were mess, failure, death, mistakes, and the people I hated, including myself." ~ Anne Lamott

9

RELEASING OBLIGATION

"Let go or be dragged." ~ Zen Proverb

To heal, we must construct new contracts. But, before we can construct them, we must tackle the broken ideas we've been holding about expectations, shame, martyrdom, and niceness. Why do I say they're "broken ideas?" Simple. They're standing in the way of our peace and unfettered joy. We're caught holding our conceptions of what's "supposed" to be instead of seeing how that prevents us from getting what we want.

~ It's All Norman Rockwell's Fault ~

Our culture sanitizes life. It "should" be easy. Families should be this. Relationships should be that. If given a writing prompt about what "should" be, we'd have *plenty* to say. The trouble is that our expectations rarely line up with reality.

What's the true source of the pain we feel? Is it our family, or the unmet expectations we hold *about* our family? Might a different belief structure about families shift our experience? What if we didn't think that families were supposed to be supportive, loving, connected, respectful? What if we thought families were simply supposed to be structured environments to raise children? Would that diminish the pain we felt since we would no longer be disappointed? When we are members of a family that has not matched up against our "supposed to be" ideal, we feel entitled to our pain. Can we agree that expectations lead to disappointment? And disappointment equals pain, right? Well, if you remove disappointment then you remove the pain.

If I learned anything from algebra, I know that if A=B and B=C then A=C. Therefore, if expectations equal disappointment and disappointment equals pain then expectations equal pain.

Abundant with expectations, we hold judgments and resentments. We resent our jealousy and feelings of rejection. We blame others for making us feel that way, and often simultaneously judge ourselves for being weak. What if we could interpret these "ugly" emotions as part of an alarm system, alerting us to a system malfunction that needs repair? That's all they are; they are signals that your soul is sending, urging you to love yourself, to find healthy connection, to be nourished.

~ Exercise ~

Make a list of resentments and judgments that you're holding. Things that you get riled up about when thinking about people, situations, and even yourself. Whether it's how your neighbor parks in the street or how your mother speaks to you, chronicle these thoughts to bring them into the light. Once they are there, you can examine and evaluate them to decide if they make sense to remain. For each, ask:

"Does this serve me?"

"How could I change it so it would?"

Resentment has no power. It's inert poison. It dulls you and your ability to grow, evolve, and bring beauty into the world. On the other hand, anger has energy and purpose. Anger tells us that something needs to change, to move on. That we need to act on something. If anger is tied to these resentments, then it's high time to examine it and pair it with an action in response to the emotion. Sometimes that means addressing a lack of boundaries in a relationship. Other times it means having tough conversations that are long overdue. Often it necessitates forgiveness of ourselves or others so that we can leave the anger WITH the events instead of carrying them forward in the form of resentment (and shame, if our resentment is internalized and directed at ourselves).

Do you know how I know that resentment has no power to do anything constructive? Because if it did, things would have gone my ex-husband's way as far as I was concerned a looooonnnnnng time ago. The same holds true for people in your life, whether you're the resent-er or the resent-ee. When have you ever known the feeling of resentment to create positive change in anyone or anything? I'll tell you when: Never. So, if for no other reason than that, knock it off already.

Imagine for a moment that you're traveling down the road and you spot a turtle crossing into traffic. You feel compelled to help it across, so you leap from your vehicle and pick it up. Once safely to the other side, you start thinking that Mr. Turtleman (or Turtlewoman…you haven't gotten that far) would be safer off in the nearby woods where there might be a stream and more cover. Mr. Turtleman starts biting you, over and over again. You're bleeding, but you're convinced of your plan, so you keep going. The stream you envisioned isn't appearing anytime soon and Mr. Turtleman is getting more and more injurious with his snapping at your flesh. You aren't one to give up once you've committed to a course of action, so on you trudge, leaving crime-scene levels of blood trailing behind you.

Holding onto resentment and judgment feels a lot like that: You know it's hurting you, but you've convinced yourself that being right outweighs any other consideration. Remember that you don't have to prove the person who is at the other end of your injury was wrong in order to honor the pain or injury you experienced. For example, a parent could have levied a punishment that was "warranted" but you still were left with damage. It could have been "justified" without it serving you well. It can be both injurious AND understandable.

On the other hand, it might have been downright criminal AND you can still let it go. You can know that the act of holding onto it is bringing darkness into your spirit and you have committed to a life of light.

Because that's what a Pain Rebel does.

~ Chains of Obligation ~

"People show you who they are.
Believe them the first time." ~ Maya Angelou

Note that Maya Angelou said, "believe them" not "hold contempt for them." We don't have to keep punishing them. That takes soooo much energy. When we punish others, we often punish ourselves…and vice versa. The more I beat myself up for being where I am, the longer I'm going to stay. Same goes for others. The longer we harp on others for their faults, the deeper the grooves of judgment and resentment.

There's one surefire and simple way to lose 90% of your judgments and resentments:

Drop the word "should" from your vocabulary.

"Should" will break your heart…and spirit. How can a word be that potent? Easy. Should carries with it the broken promise of expectation. From the way we look at life to how we manage our most personal relationships, our instinctual clutching to shoulds puts our happiness in the hands of others. Assumptions are synonymous with shoulds. How? They are rich with expectations because they exist in our heads, unchecked or challenged by the people who have the agency to satisfy or disappoint us. Do you want to be a shame/guilt receptacle? Then stop opening the lid to your spirit.

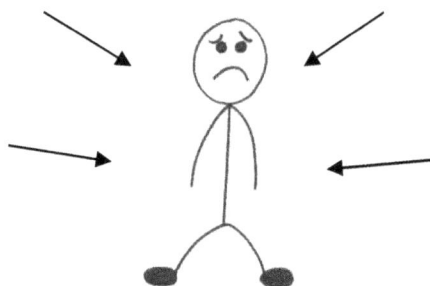

Shoulds showing up as **shame,** coming at us and being internalized.

Shoulds showing up as **resentment,** coming from us towards others.

Shoulds enact a shame-resentment dynamic. If you "should" yourself, you'll feel shame when you fall short. If you "should" others, you'll resent them for letting you down. Shoulds remove your power, locking you into a victim stance. You have no power over what others decide to do, and frankly, shoulds don't hold any allure to get us off the dime. Shoulds just fill the space where action could exist, poisoning our relationship with ourselves and other people. Far too many of my clients get caught in a "shame cyclone" where one regret creates more and more and more of them until they feel swept away by that toxic feeling.

Let's say they say something regrettable to someone they care about. Instead of working to resolve it in a healthy and timely manner, they shut the other person out, drowning themselves in self-recrimination. That practice gets them eating and drinking to excess. Then they feel shitty about how they look, so they are crabby with everyone they meet. Those embarrassing outbursts bring more shame, and it goes on and on and on.

Sound familiar? It's time to investigate where you're holding expectations and shame so you can hop out of that energy-sucking vortex of bullshit.

What are the "shoulds" that you are living by and placing as expectations on others? In other words, what do you think you're supposed to be doing? What do you expect others do be doing?

Where do you notice shame in your life? Are you ashamed of any pattern, relationship, or circumstance in your life? Where do you hide what's really going on from others, or from yourself?

Who are the people who keep disappointing you?

How We Take Our POWER Back

There is a deep and lasting pain that comes from expecting more from (and believing in) someone more than they do in themselves. This sets us up to do battle with a shadow, an imaginary or hopeful person instead of the human standing right in front of us. It drains our energy and our state of mind. As my former trainer once said (about clients she'd had to fire in the past): I can't care more about your fat ass than you do. Amen. We can't weaponize our "shoulds" to try to control other people's investment in their own lives.

And we need to drop the should from our own narrative. Think of the "plan" you had for your life. What was that? Who contrived it? Did you feel passion for it? The best advice I ever received when I was caught in a loop, revisiting the plan I had for my life was: Fuck the plan. Was I happy? Was my life interesting? Was I living out loud and with love? If so, then fuck the plan. I let go of the "should be" version of my life and grabbed onto the "what is" truth. That was a *gift*. I sat fully in the present moment and acknowledged my joy for it. I wanted everything in my life; and the stuff that was missing, I got to choose to pursue. I agreed to my own, intentional plan.

In our relationships (personal or professional), we can establish similar accountability through agreement instead of building resentment (and superiority). We set people up for failure all the damn time, practically living in should-ville. "They should know. They should do such-and-such. They should be x-y-z."

But have they **agreed** to live up to those standards? If not, you'll be deeply aggravated (and *exhausted*) trying to get them to live up to your standards. You'll get wedged in resentment and disappointment, dampening your power. In short:

Want = *Responsibility*

Should = *Shame & Resentment*

There's a huge and discernible difference between responsibility and shame or guilt. Responsibility is a signal to do something. Shame and resentment simply keep us calcified in the past by tethering us to what happened, what we did. Responsibility keeps us anchored in the present toward an influenced future. Responsibility is steeped in power. Shame and resentment are smothered in victimhood. In those emotions we are victims of ourselves *and* others. In order to step fully into our power, we must break with our histories.

And those histories are bursting with old contracts.

New contracts bring us into a different, brighter future.

How are you supposed to do *that?* Move from "should" to "want to?" It's a true power move. How? Because you aren't squandering your power by getting mixed up in things that aren't yours to change. You're deciding that you want something and that, my friends, has muscle behind it. If you say you *should* have a salad for lunch, would you drive far to get it? Nope. If you say you *want* one, can you say the same? Nope. You'd hop right in your car and get it.

When we say we **want** something, we instinctively take responsibility for making it happen. When we say that we **should do** something, we find ourselves stalled, stuck, and if we take any action at all, it follows a sluggish path. Want an example? (Yeah, I saw that I did that right there...)

Current statement: "They should show up on time."

New statement: "I want them to show up on time."

Current statement: "I shouldn't feel that way."

New statement: "I don't want to feel that way."

When we make this simple language replacement, we offer up a profound shift in how we relate to a situation, other people, and ourselves. When we say "want," we are communicating a desire, one that we are invited to take ownership of and attempt to fulfill. If we are passionate about making it happen, we have two clear choices:

1. If the outcome is in our control, we can own our desire and push the language change one step further and say, "I will." Using weight loss as an example, our current statement might be, "I shouldn't be so fat." Our new statement (using "want") would shift to "I don't want to be so fat." Our new and improved action statement might sound like, "I will not be fat (anymore)."
2. If the outcome is NOT in our control, we can still own our desire and try to hammer out a new agreement with the person(s) in control. For example, if it's our friend who is late to things, instead of standing in judgment of them being late (resulting in tension and resentment) we could negotiate out an agreement that allows them to commit to making a change (and/or you adjusting your expectations) to create more relationship harmony.

Coming from our wants...and creating *agreements* where we used to hold *expectations*...requires that we communicate clearly and honestly. When we ask for things in a roundabout way, we get responses in a roundabout way. When we ask for things in a direct way, we get responses in a direct way...or at the very least, we have set the stage for a direct conversation. That's the way healthy relationships work.

And having healthy relationships starts with the one we have with ourselves. When we make the self-defeating mistake of turning a "should" into a "have to," we lock ourselves into patterns of behavior that rob us of our agency. We say, "I should do this" and slide down the slippery slope into "I have to do this."

As a self-described cage rattler, I'm not afraid to shake up the status quo. Here's a statement that always gets quite a reaction from my audiences:

There is absolutely nothing I ever have to do.

What? Of course there is! You have to pay your bills and take care of your kids and….and…. and.

Nope.

You don't *have to* do any of those things. You don't even have to eat. If you come right down to it, you don't even have to breathe. Every last damn thing you do is a choice, whether conscious or otherwise. There are no "have to" things in this life. Sure, lots of choices come with hefty consequences. Nevertheless, they are **choices**. Acknowledge this and free yourself from the illusion of obligation and the delusion that you don't *always* have choice. You do. Always, always, always. Sometimes they are shitty choices, but they are always *choices*. And choice equals power. In order to choose, we have to see the choice, of course, so that's why our first job is **awareness**.

Before I became aware of how "should" and "have to" show up in relationship dynamics, I had a huge issue with trust. I thought things should be a certain way, but they never were. Like you, I'd been hurt in the past and vowed to never let it happen it again. But it did happen, over and over again. So, what did I do? I trusted less and less as time went on, of course. I was left feeling anxious and resentful. Broken, really, and destined to have dissatisfying, dysfunctional (sometimes abusive) relationships. I expected things to go along with all the "shoulds" I had in my head. Shocker: They never did.

When I was able to see the ways in which I agreed to be a certain way and tolerate a certain manner of behavior from others, a magical thing happened that changed my life forever: My expectations about others started to equal reality. Let me say that again, realllllllly slowly and loudly for the people in the back:

Expectations equaled reality.

I wasn't falling from the tower of expectations onto the cold, hard ground of reality. They were one and the same. My expectations reflected reality. I let go of my "shoulds" and saw things as they were. I wasn't infusing reality with hope and what I wanted. I expected what I was likely to get. My lesson: Watch what people do; pay very little attention to what they say.

Please don't misunderstand me: This process is *not* about lowering your expectations; it's about *righting* them. You can trust absolutely everyone…To be who they are, in the situation they are in, conditions they are under, and within the contract they signed. Putting our *expectations* on others instead of simply *observing* them gets in the way of our happiness and initiates all kinds of stress.

Believe me, I have screwed this up plenty of times in the years since I had this epiphany. I have this pesky little thing called "hope" that gets in the way. I *hope* that people will be who I need them to be instead of who they are. I let my hope for my needs getting met (someday?) to eclipse what the person is likely to do. What's that saying? "Inspect before you expect." You can better align expectations with reality when you're informed and aren't blinded by hope.

Character is demonstrated by actions, not words. Watch what people do…it's very revealing. When someone tells you that you are important to them and that they value things about you that their other relationships don't offer, but then they opt to spend their time and resources on those other relationships, believe their actions. It might sound nicer in their head to say that they value the things they say they do, but the truth is revealed in their actions…and in yours. Who and where you are in life is reflected in who you spend the most time with and invest the most energy in. Be careful. As Atticus told us, "We will carry the pieces of all those who have built and broken us." If they aren't choosing you, will you choose them?

Here's a visual to keep in mind the next time you're tempted to expect someone to be someone who you want them to be versus who they've shown themselves to be:

EXPECTATIONS

↓

REALITY

The Gap =
Disappointment &
Loss of Trust

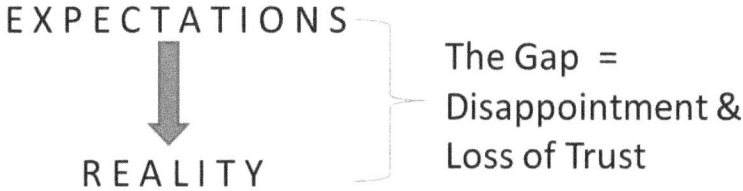

The fall from expectation to reality hurts. We call it "disappointment." How much does it hurt when someone calls you a "disappointment?" Or tells you that you've disappointed them? It's hard to hear. It means we've fallen from grace. How do we get ourselves tangled up in these disappointments over and over again? It goes back to trust and understanding. When I say "trust" I mean choosing how much you should trust. When I say "understanding" I don't mean blind compassion and being a doormat. I mean using your trust muscle the way it was meant to be used:

By trusting people to be who they are, where they are.

If you trust your best friend to be chummy with you in the workplace when she's targeting a big promotion, you're going to feel let down. Did she not act like a friend? Perhaps not the friend she is to you outside of work, but that's not a bad thing. She's different in work because her priorities are different there based on her choices and desires: To be a professional success. She might jump in front of a moving train for you when you're socializing in the city on the weekend. But if she's professionally ambitious, make no mistake: She might be just this side of cordial at the office if she perceives that anything beyond that may be seen as unprofessional.

Set your expectations right: Life will be easier as a Pain Rebel, not easy. There will always be problems that come your way. Problems just change form and intensity. The critical shift is that *you* will be different. You'll be stronger, clearer, happier, lighter, and more intentional. To quote Shakespeare, "Expectation is the root of all heartache."

The truth is messy and life itself is messy. People are messy. Very few things are ever neat and tidy. We've been raised to believe that messy equals tragic. As Pain Rebels, we have to get comfy in the messy. And some of that messy includes the way to speak about, and to, ourselves.

~ Watching Our Words ~

Language is very powerful. When we define ourselves in strict terms ("I'm a big picture guy," "I'm the rebellious type," "I'm indecisive," "I'm impulsive"), we limit our available responses to a given situation. The word "always" is inferred in such a definition. It IS, we ARE, as we describe it. I have a rule in my coaching work: Clients must agree to eliminate "always" and "never" and replace with "sometimes" in their vocabulary. Doing so opens their minds to possibilities. I find that when challenged, everyone can come up with an example of when they didn't do what they said they "always" do so it just isn't an accurate word.

As an example, I have a client who described herself as an indecisive person. When I probed, I discovered that this wasn't the case. She gets up out of bed in the morning. She then chooses a long list of personal hygiene products/practices, chooses her clothing and which style to sport, selects her radio station favorites...the list goes on and on. All of these selections require decisions among an endless stream of choices. Is she really an indecisive person? Or does she struggle to make *certain* decisions? When we realized that the latter was true, we tackled the particular triggers in those areas that made it tougher for her to be decisive in *those* areas.

**She was stuck in old contracts,
contracts that limited her view of herself and the world.**

If she had kept defining herself so narrowly, she would have likely continued to opt out of circumstances where she would have been asked to make decisions. Imagine how limiting her life would have been? Don't limit yourself or other people by defining them (or yourself) with those big blanketing statements. Challenge your assumptions and definitions. Ready to assess that?

What are the things that you say are "always" true about you?

When are they *not* true about you? When do you do something that doesn't fit that "always" category?

Notice anything about the places you are and aren't like that? In front of certain people? When you're at work versus at home? What differences do you see?

When you figure out where you are displaying the characteristic that you want to do more of, you can do more of it in other places. Isn't that great? We can start seeing that we already are where we wish to be, at least part of the way. We are just witnessing what we've *been*. Our only error has been using the wrong words to define who we are and what we do.

Yep. We are responsible for our own limitations. We are responsible for our own tethering to an existence that reduces our space in the world. "I'm impulsive" can serve to excuse certain reckless behaviors, but that's not the whole story. True, extreme impulsivity is dangerous (walking into traffic), so not many people are truly "impulsive" all of the time. They live within limits. They obey the law. They exist within a structure or myriad ones. They do act impulsively *at times.* At other times they don't. They live on a spectrum, venturing into the outer limits at times. All of us have the capacity to embody any behavior at any point on the spectrum. It is all about choice. Confidence. Intention. Risk.

We concluded that what you did yesterday (and all those other pesky yesterdays) got you to where you are today, so it follows that if you want to be someplace else in the future, you'll need to start making decisions that are consistent with that future vision of yourself. What *is* your future vision of yourself? Shall we get started with your vision of where and how you'd like to be…and how that differs from where and how you find yourself? Without tackling these ingredients, you'll just be bouncing between the guardrails of life.

~ Exercise ~

Write down five words that best describe you.

How do you know those are the words that fit? What behaviors of yours demonstrate those characteristics?

Which one(s) of these are you proud of? Which one(s) do you try to hide?

Do you want the five words to be different? What would they be if there was no work involved?

How can you show yourself and others that's who you want to be?

Hold onto these with statements everything that you are; if you don't, you'll lose yourself as sure as the sun will rise in the sky in the morning.

~ Martyrdom Competitions ~

We perceive and treat pain as a badge of honor. Have you ever fought for bragging rights as to who of you and your co-worker/friend has suffered more? It might look something like this:

Person 1: "OMG, can you believe Brad left all his work for me when he left on vacation? What a jerk. Now I'm going to spend the next week working late nights to make sure it all gets done. I'm so stressed."

Person 2: "You think THAT'S bad? My boss was supposed to hire a person to replace Stephanie and she still hasn't done it, so I've been covering for her for SIX WEEKS! I haven't been home till after dinner in over a month!"

Person 1: "Yeah, but you could push back to your boss on that since it's her fault that the position is open. My boss loves Brad so if I even THINK of criticizing him, I'm toast. Plus, I've been fighting this head cold for a month. My immune system is SHOT."

Person 2: "Well, at least you don't get migraines. It's so painful I can hardly focus at times. Plus, your kids are cute. Mine are *teenagers*."

Person 1: "Cute? Sure, but they need to be driven everywhere and they're constantly forgetting one thing or another so I'm always racing around trying to fix things."

Person 2: …….

And so it goes. We suffer to fit in, to stay connected to others who are held in suffering.

Have you ever been told that you shouldn't leave a relationship and you're threatened with, "No one will ever love you like I do." It sounds scary until you listen to that again. How ARE they loving you? Is it healthy? Is it abundant? Is it nurturing? Is it respectful? If not, then I certainly hope no one will ever love you like THAT. You deserve better.

My hope is that your new contracts will reflect a refreshing accountability, a freedom from a victim or martyr stance and the drama inherent in both.

~ You're Not Nice ~

How many times have you agreed to something out of perceived obligation, or because you didn't want to rock the boat? Maybe you've done it so regularly that you consider yourself a "nice person?" Well, I hate to be the one to break it to you, but it's not nice to say "yes" and not mean it. Why? Because your heart isn't in it so you're probably not:

~ The best person for the job/assignment, and/or

~ Going to enjoy yourself, so you'll build resentment.

I know nice and that ain't it. Think can't say "no?" Consider yourself "nice" because you always say "yes?" You're not being nice. You're building resentments, judgments, holding grudges. You're failing to have integrity because you're not saying or doing what you mean. Integrity comes with great risk; the risk of being misunderstood, judged, or rejected. Instead, you're playing a role. You're playing it safe. You're turning yourself inside out for others then holding them responsible for how shitty and burdened you feel. Wow. Sound nice to you? Not so much. My advice?

Say "yes" with genuine enthusiasm or say "no" with great regard.

If you mean "yes," say it. If you mean "no," convey it, with genuine care and concern for yourself, the other person, and the relationship.

~ Concluding Thoughts~

This chapter was a wake-up call to all the "nice," compliant, dutiful people who are miserable on the inside and haven't quite known why. Now you do, so what, pray tell, are you going to do about it?

Key Chapter Concepts

- Our expectations lead to misery.
- Shoulds create expectations, shame, and resentment.
- Wants manifest responsibility and agreements.
- Martyrs love misery.
- "Nice" doesn't mean what you think it does.

"You can't spend your whole life holding the door open for people and then being angry they didn't thank you. Nobody asked you to hold the fucking door." ~ Alex Vause in "Orange is the New Black"

10

CONTRACTS WORKSHOP

"When we are no longer able to change a situation, we are challenged to change ourselves." ~ Viktor Frankl

When you get to the point where you're tired of or overwhelmed by the same old, same old, it's time to take stock of your contracts.

Remember, contracts are the viewpoints we've been abiding by that have created the relationships and circumstances we now find ourselves in. For so long, we imagined that if we did what our contracts told us was right and good, then we would reap all sorts of benefits. We'd have love, fortune, and *approval.* Only, that's not how things have happened, have they? All good things *aren't* waiting on the other side of you clinging to these contracts. You're suffering and, truth be told, you're the only one who can do anything about it.

So, what *do* you do? Review your core beliefs, then challenge them. How do you know what your core beliefs are? Let's see, shall we? I'll leave a little room for you to make some notes, but I recommend that you get some paper to jot down your thoughts.

Question 1 (Guiding Principles): What do you *believe* about life's core elements? Is love supposed to hurt, be your savior, or somewhere in between? Is work how you define yourself or is it a means to an end? Before I put words into your head, I'll leave you to it....

Love:

Sex:

Family:

Parenting:

Friendship:

Success:

Work:

Wealth:

Health:

Don't cheat. If you haven't written at least one guiding principle you have about each of the above terms, stop reading and do that right now.

Yes, right now.

If you have trouble coming up with something, phone a friend. Ask your spouse. If you do, phrase your question carefully: "What do I say I believe about X?" Why am I being so specific? I have my reasons...

You're done? Alrighty then. It's time for step two. Now, take the list you made and now answer the following for each statement you made for each of the terms (love, sex, family, parenting, friendship, success, work, wealth, health):

Question 2 (Behavior): How do I *demonstrate* that this is what I believe? How do people know that this is what I believe? If I couldn't *tell* them and could only *show* them, how would they know it was true about me?

Did you have a hard time coming up with an answer for each term? Were some terms harder than others? Which ones? Do you have insight as to why that might be?

I have a guess. I heard a quote once that has stayed with me when it comes to human *values* versus human *behavior*:

If you want to know what people value, don't ask them; simply watch how they spend their money and their time.

As human beings, we like to think that we value certain things because it's either what we *want to* believe or what we think we *should* believe and value.

The problem is that our behavior is often very different.

Or our behavior is exactly what we say we believe, but we hate the idea of believing that. Need an example?

Let's take an easy one: Health.

Question 1 (*guiding principle*): Health is important to me. I value nutrition, exercise, and regular check-ups. Without our health, nothing else matters.

Question 2 (*behavior consistent with guiding principle*): [Crickets....]

Struggle: My behavior doesn't match my guiding principle. I eat a diet high in refined foods and sugars, I don't exercise regularly, and I prioritize many things over my health.

What gives?

Old contracts.

Our new, (unwritten) contracts are consistent with our *guiding principles*. But our old contracts are consistent with our *behavior*. Our new, (unwritten) contracts represent where we *want to be* whereas our old contracts account for where we've *been* and where we *are*.

Why do we need to look at our old contracts? Because they explain the origin of our behavior and why we are struggling to make changes or live in joy. We have to identify which habits to break by making the unconscious, conscious.

How do we figure out what our old contracts are?

Well, our behavior gave us some clues. Go back to the last exercise we just did and list out how you *behave* in relation to each term. For example, for my health, I'd say:

I eat a diet high in refined foods and sugars, I don't exercise regularly, and I prioritize many things over my health.

What do your answers for each look like? Notice anything interesting? Are you happy with the responses? Which ones are working, and which ones aren't?

Now that you've seen where you have *guiding principles* that are different from your *behavior*, it's time to clean up that discrepancy.

What are the beliefs that your behaviors indicate that you *actually* believe?

Going back to my health example, my behavior would say that I *actually* believe that:

I'm likely not going to live long. My parents didn't. If I work too hard at being healthy, I will be less like them every day. Being unlike them will mean that I'm disloyal to them. If I'm meant to be healthy it'll just happen regardless of what I do.

Yikes!

What the hell do I do with *that*??

The same thing *you're* going to do. Challenge each and every one of your behaviors that indicate you have a belief that isn't what you want it to be. You're also going to challenge the self-limiting beliefs that you've been putting right out front. How you've been acting in self-destructive ways.

Your life is a result of the contracts you've made and those that you're keeping.

Want a different life? Let's get down to business then.

Turn back to the list you made as we kicked off this chapter. What are the beliefs that *limit* you, standing in the way of the life you *want to have* versus the life you *find yourself in*? (Yes, you'll need more paper! And, yes, you may need to phone a friend for assistance!)

Love:

Sex:

Family:

Parenting:

Friendship:

Success:

Work:

Wealth:

Health:

Start with targeting the big, instrumental ones that are standing in your way of living an authentic, joyful, abundant life. Up to this point, you've been loyal. Loyal to what?

Loyal to a pact you made with pain. What? Why would you have made a pact with pain?

Because you didn't…you couldn't…know better.

Examining the old and creating the new contracts is strategic and takes our innocent ignorance into account. We strategically evaluate each contract we signed early on, knowing that we now have awareness and choice that we didn't have early on. We have it *now*. Our old contracts kept us bound to our original, core wound by carrying it into the future. Now that we are aware, we have a duty to update them.

Want some real satisfaction? Put your old contracts into a dumpster fire. If you want to be more constructive about it, hold a symbolic burning ceremony, watching the ashes rise…as you soon will.

~ Writing New Contracts ~

Now comes the fun: Rewriting our contracts so they **serve** versus *limit* us!

Speaking of limits, the sky is the limit with our new contracts. Now that we are holding the pen, we get to write contracts that reflect our greatest hopes and aspirations. We want wild, passionate, doting love? We get to define "love" that way! We want success to mean something other than sacrificing everything else in our lives for it? That's our call!

Does writing new contracts mean that the qualities that you value about yourself have to change? Absolutely not. You can define yourself the same way (loving, loyal, giving, strong) but **exhibit** those same qualities differently. Personally, I would describe myself in many of the same ways at 16 as at 48 but HOW I do those things is very different. "Loyal" can mean something different. Being "loving" can hold new truths. To make an old, outdated contract better, redefine desirable qualities that are exhibited through new behaviors. Success can come at a lesser cost.

Rewriting your contracts has five core components:

1. Quality Expressed: The aspect about myself that I want to believe is true and I want the world to think about me.

2. Old Contract: Remember, you find this by looking at your *behavior* around aspects about yourself, relationships, and the world to indicate what you really believe.

3. Meaning/Terms: What are the implications of your Old Contract? What's the underlying message about you, others, or life that abiding by this contract communicates?

4. Benefits: What are you getting out of this? Safety? Compassion? Pity? Attention? Connection? There is always a benefit, even with the worst of circumstances. We are all benefitting from pain whether we choose to acknowledge it or not.

5. New Contract: What is another way I could express that quality about myself without creating unnecessary pain and suffering? How could I live more honestly and courageously?

Time to explore this process. Let's say I describe myself as "loving." Here's how my process might look:

Quality Expressed: I am loving.

Old Contract: I suffer for others.

Meaning/Terms: Suffering equals love.

Benefits: Others can be lazy; I can remain hidden and martyr myself.

New Contract: I love freely by having excess love, by loving myself first.

When we rewrite our contracts, we might find ourselves wandering aimlessly in the woods of thought, unsure of where we want to land. What does happiness really mean? How can we define love? Loyalty? Success? These are big questions that demand clear answers. In order to get to clarity, we must accept that our wandering has a purpose, a deeply critical one: It demonstrates that the world is your oyster. You are not obligated to hold any particular belief structure; you are free to choose one of your liking. As you review, add to, and subtract from your brainstorming, you'll likely settle on language that suits you and your development. If you don't, start where you began: in the old contracts' territory.

If loyalty meant "suffering so that others wouldn't feel discomfort," you can write a new contract in opposition to that but still express your loyalty. The new contract might be "loyalty means being supportive of the growth and development of my loved ones, being truthful with them, even if it might cause them discomfort."

If success meant "working yourself to the bone," you can write a new contract that states, "success means being happy *in* a moment instead of in pursuit *of* a moment."

Can you see how in both cases you can be **what** you want to be without doing it **how** you used to do it?

Going forward, when you notice a response of thought, feeling, or action, ask yourself if it's the old contract that you're operating under?

If so, REJECT. If it's the new contract: KEEP.

I made that sound waaaaaaay too easy.

How We Take Our POWER Back

If you're anything like me, you go to the gym for a day or two and you're befuddled that you're not in shape already. Clearly, to be in strong, fit condition, it takes routine and devotion to the practice.

The same holds true for our contracts.

Revisit your new contracts daily. Keeping them at the forefront of your mind empowers you because you demonstrate their priority in delivering a sunnier life. This habit supports you in being intentional about how you think, feel, and behave. You shift your mental models by updating, then abiding by, your contracts. You manifest the best aspect of true rebellion: Deciding that the choices others made for you can only be ousted by choices you make for yourself. No one gets to control you but *you*. How do you control yourself?

Operate under contracts that *you* write and honor.

"It's you against you every day.
Make sure the right you wins." ~ Jason Shurgot

~ People ~

What do you do about the people you've been keeping these contracts with? The lovers, friends, co-workers, family members.

People you've attracted into your life help you to keep your contracts. They aren't the enemy, they are simply contract keepers. By helping you maintain the status quo, they've done exactly as they were contracted to do. You don't need to hate or blame them.

People are guides, mirrors, or reminders.

Choose them wisely.

Each person we meet simply challenge us to choose between them and committing to our new contracts.

What's it going to be?

Pain Rebel

~ Vigilance ~

Vigilance is required to hold the change, to adhere to the new contracts. At the bottom of our new contracts, we must write:

I take action on my contracts.

If we don't commit to them, they won't take hold and we'll quickly slip back into our old, outdated contracts. How can we know that they are "new contract"-worthy? Do they empower you to be?

~ A power agent (not victim of person or circumstance)?
~ Worthy?
~ Abundant (in all senses of the word)?
~ Perfectly imperfect?

We must stand in constant vigilance against sliding back into our old contracts. They were strong and firm and held us hostage in their dysfunction for a long time. Just like with addicts, when we are too confident (almost cocky) is when we are likely to get clobbered with our old patterning. Practicing presence, not judging any feelings – just being aware and accepting of them – puts us in a position to see when an old contract is rearing its ugly head and hijacking our experience. When we notice ourselves feeling emotional, overwhelmed, and TRIGGERED, it ought to serve as an alarm system that we're aligning with an old contract.

Think of a train ride. When we arrive at our old stop, it's okay to take a look around, to see what still feels familiar. Just don't bring your bags off and proclaim, "Oh, goodie! I live here now!" Over time, you won't feel drawn to get off the train and look around. There's nothing for you there. Soon enough, you'll be satisfied to simply look out the window with the confidence that you don't belong there.

Know this: It applies to me, too. I found myself in a familiar spot with a man who had wandered in and out of my life over the years, awakening me to the truth that my old contracts were seeping in, telling me outdated stories about who I was and what I deserved. So, I wrote my contracts down – both the old and the new. The result was mind-blowing and life changing.

My old contracts (what I was **BOUND to**):

~ I suffer anything for love.
~ I always take them back, no matter how they've treated me in the past.
~ I am not chosen when there's competition with another lover.
~ I am with those who are broken and damaged because I am, too, and it is my duty to save and fix them.
~ I can never hold onto a man for very long. Love always disappears.
~ I am loved at times, but the love always leaves.
~ I am too much for those I love so they eventually (or quickly) leave.
~ I strive to be the best partner, lover, friend, temptress, I can be, but it's never enough.
~ Love always exists in the shadows. I am unworthy of public coupling, of being bragged about.
~ The love that lasts longest is the love that is never returned.

My new contracts (what I **CHOOSE** for myself):

~ I am worthy of lasting, committed, devoted, passionate, strong, public love.
~ I send love to all people, but I share love only with those who are worthy of my love's great gift.
~ I choose only those who choose me.
~ I am whole and complete and am in relationship with those who mirror me.
~ People may come and go freely from my life but those capable of love are the only ones I allow into my inner sanctum.

~ I am abundant and only seek others who are equally abundant.

~ Love grows in abundance.

~ Love exists in me – and IS me – so it is always present and overflowing.

~ Love is something to be proud of sharing.

~ I am worthy of being bragged about, defended, protected, pampered, and loved passionately and enduringly. I give that love and receive that love.

~ My needs matter in love.

Like I said, life changing.

What if we don't know if we want or believe in something or not? Maybe we are given advice to adopt a new contract, but we aren't sure we want to follow or reject? Put it in the "maybe later" zone. Record it and revisit it down the road to see if your passions are chasing it into the "want" zone. You have to *want* your new contract in order for it to be valuable.

Remember: You're in charge of you. Act like it.

Other times we know what we want but we lack passionate energy. Maybe we *want* to believe in ourselves, but we don't. We want to have new contracts that aren't self-defeating but when we write down healthier versions, our bullshit detector goes berserk. Clients the world over have asked me, "What if I don't believe the new contracts but I hate the old ones?" It's like waiting for motivation to go to the gym before working out. Fitness coaches don't recommend waiting for the brain to lead the way; instead, they'll tell you to just get up and go to the gym, confident that once you get there and the endorphins kick in, you'll be happy you did. The same holds true for following new contracts: Act upon them before you fully believe that they apply to you and see what happens. See how you level up your relationships. Witness your self-perception shift with how you treat yourself.

How We Take Our POWER Back

~ Exercise ~

Notice when you're following an old contract and, instead, choose an action consistent with your *new* contract. Alternatively, when you find yourself doing something you're proud of, consider which new contract you're following to get to this feel-good moment.

What was different about that moment?

What do you credit this better feeling or experience with?

Following this practice has solid benefits: It increases your awareness, strengthens your commitment to your new contracts, and helps you avoid a slide back into your old patterns of behavior. Because who wants *that?*

~ The Sucky Part ~

Becoming acutely aware of our contracts isn't all good. The messy underbelly of it can knock you right off track if you're not ready to take an honest look at yourself in the mirror and take responsibility for the part you've played in the contracts you've constructed. True, some of them you signed before you knew what was happening. Plus, the things you agreed to early on tend to look similar to what you continued to agree to, especially when you weren't conscious about your power to reconstruct your agreements.

As a result, we wake up one day and realize that we've built a life of accommodating to others, to living out some form of self-abuse by not co-creating relationships in a healthy manner. We've been telling the sad, sad story of our lives to anyone who will listen, or simply communicating it through the life we've been living.

We end up steeped in anger at others for how they've taken advantage of us, yet the truth beneath that is much uglier: We let them do it. We offered up our sanity on a silver platter for their consumption. We mistakenly believe that when they do A, we *must* do B. That's the dance of the contract. But, when we do B (and it's not a healthy pattern), it makes us upset, and this upsettedness leads to a nasty creature:

Resentment.

Resentment is poison. It destroys relationships. It steals our joy. Avoiding it is possible only when we resist getting drawn back into our old contracts.

The last line of defense when you find yourself playing out the script of your old contracts is to ask yourself, "What else could be true here?" You're apt to shortcut right into your old contracts by believing what you've always believed about yourself, other people, and the world. Your new contracts challenge those shortcuts. So, give yourself a break for being efficient! Of COURSE you'd respond that way. Of COURSE you'd be reactive and take the quickest path. Of COURSE you'd be lured back into old ways of thinking and feeling by your old contracts. It's ok. This is a process. Be gentle with yourself.

Imagine a child climbing on your lap, seeking the comfort of someone stronger, smarter, and more resourceful. Can you ever imagine telling them that they were unworthy or bad…or anything that your old contracts told you about yourself? Never! We'd affirm how *enough* they were by just being themselves. We'd fill them with love, hope, and support. We'd remind them of their worthiness for greatness and abundance.

But you see, you **are** that child. And now you are this adult. You were always deserving of love. Protection. Support. Even if…especially if…you didn't receive it. Both things are true:

You deserved the best treatment.

AND

You didn't receive it.

How We Take Our POWER Back

Just because you deserved it doesn't mean you received it. Just because you didn't receive it doesn't mean you didn't deserve it. On the contrary: You were born deserving of unlimited love, protection, and support. You didn't have to be pretty or smart or talented. You didn't have to earn it in any way, shape, or form. Let me say it one more time in case you missed it.

YOU WERE BORN DESERVING.

So many of us were parented by emotional children who had limited bandwidth to really care for us. Our parents often meant well but they just didn't fill the cracks in our spirits. It's time for us to do that for ourselves now.

It's never too late to heal that child inside. That time is now.

If you'd benefit from a deep dive into this inner child affirmation work, I recommend my book, *Little Landslides* (2016) and the letters I wrote back to "little Bridget."

"Experience taught her. Hurt raised her.
Neither defined her." ~ Adrian Michael

146

11

HOW WE HEAL

"Time smooths the jagged edges of our emotions." ~ James Kask

Love. We were built for love. Our tender humanity craves love and connection. Pain takes hold when love fails us or when we fail love. When we aren't seen, understood, or honored. When we feel let down by others, disregarded. When they leave us – by death or by decision. When they reject us, personally or professionally. When they fail to see our worth. We innately know the difference between feeling cared about and not; it doesn't matter if it's a lover, friend, coworker, neighbor, family member, or a stranger who cut us off in traffic. At a base level, we want to feel concern from others and we experience pain when we don't.

Looking at our old contracts…and constructing our new ones…puts us in touch with both hope and sorrow. We hold hope for a better tomorrow, while still sorrowful for the patterns that sapped our joy and abundance for the many years it took us to get to this point.

So how do we move past this sense of loss and navigate a path to healing? Keep reading.

How We Take Our POWER Back

"Let us forget, with generosity,
those who cannot love us." ~ Pablo Neruda

~ Beauty of Rage ~

Rage is beautiful.

There's no end to the number of puzzled looks I get when I make that pronouncement publicly during a talk or workshop. Rage is *beautiful?* How is that possible?

Rage is different than anger. It's the supersize version, typically rooted in pain that doesn't typically belong to one moment. Rage tends to be the cumulative effect of a series of traumas or hurts that get stored. When there's no acceptable resolution, the feelings get buried...compressed. That compression generates rage.

Rage is your soul screaming, "I deserve better! I was born for more!" Feel that in your cells. Your soul knows your worth even when your brain and heart have forgotten.

Give yourself permission to feel the rage. It's your right. Acting on the rage? That's a different matter. I've long told my kids that it's okay to feel any way you feel but you don't get to act however you want to act. Using your rage to hurt others isn't okay; but using your rage to heal yourself is much more than okay. If you misuse it and injure others with it then YOU will be on the hook asking for forgiveness. And that's fine, but why fill the wrong side of your ledger more than you have to?

Rage can be scary. When it's coursing through your veins, it might be the most alive you've ever felt. So how do you prevent rage from hijacking you? You get angry, feel the anger, and *address* the anger when things actually happen. You shed those feelings as they arise because you know that collections ought to be reserved for stamps and coins, not feelings. Collected anger becomes rage.

Once you break free from the people and places that injured you, once you create your own safety, I want you to let that shit go. Because if you hang onto it, it will poison you. It will mute and distort your beauty. And…they will win by dominating your future like they did your past.

If you didn't want them to take your past, why would you give away your present and future?

Get angry about that possibility. Get mad that it happened. Why? It communicates that you matter(ed). It says that you see that you were a victim, but you refuse to stay there. Let it bubble up inside of you in stirring rebellion. But remember: Anger serves you…until it doesn't. It feeds your need for validation ("this happened to me") and control (puts you in charge of your healing process). It's a critical part of healing, but it's only the first half of the equation.

~ How Rage Saved My Life ~

Once I stopped wanting to die, I learned how to live.

The first time someone raped me, I wasn't old enough to fight back. I wasn't even old enough to spoon feed myself. I told a therapist once that my dad was my first sexual partner, unable to comprehend the toxic narrative that revealed about my sense of power and choice. He'd been hitting me since shortly after I was born, my cries fueling his insecurities and, therefore, his anger. His assaults on my mom were horrific, routine, and fully in my view, long before I held conscious memory. My mom eventually left him, physically, but the damage continued. As it does. She proved herself incapable of protecting me from him and a long line of abusers that shredded any hope of an innocent childhood.

By the time I reached my teens, I was on fire, burning from the inside out. I searched for a receptacle that could contain my confusion, sadness, and emerging rage. I only found myself. When I directed my anger at my family, they deflected it, refining the idea that everything that had ever happened to me was my doing, and undoing.

The first time I had consensual sex I was sixteen. I gave that honor to a boy who had zero capacity to give me much more than that, so it left me feeling hollow, worthless, and dirty. He was a raging drug and alcohol addict, much like the man who first claimed my body as his own fifteen years before.

Oh, Daddy.

In retrospect, aside from being an abusive (in every last way you can use that term) addict, I'm convinced that my father was mentally ill, an illness made worse by years of methamphetamine and heroin abuse. Both of my parents openly discussed their ongoing flirtation with suicide, naming me as their only reason to go on living. I performed for them at every turn, attempting to be so amazing that I'd save them from those shadow lives they led so shamelessly.

In the end, nothing I did was enough to save either one of them. But that's a story for another day.

By the time I was a high school junior, I had tried to kill myself three times.

My father continued to sexually and psychologically abuse me throughout my teen years. Tragically, he wasn't the only perpetrator who helped himself to my body. I lived in a fog, unable to decipher where the suffocating pain I felt in my chest and abdomen was coming from. It beckoned me to fill it with whatever distraction I could find. Some days it was food (or the lack thereof). Other days it was romantic interests and their continuous rejection. I fended off exhaustion with pure will, hoping that someday I'd be good enough to right this ship that kept taking on water, day after day after day. If only I could do more. Be more.

But I wasn't more. I gave my virginity to a boy who had no capacity to care about me beyond our trysts, mirroring back to me how little I mattered.

Six weeks after that boy crawled into my bed late one August evening, I overdosed on pills and booze. It was my third suicide attempt, and this one landed me in intensive care and a follow-on stay in a mental hospital for wayward teens. When I regained consciousness, the first thing I told the attending physician was that I couldn't even kill myself right. I wanted a way out of the overwhelming sadness I felt but kept running into dead end hallways. And a padded room.

I wish I could say that the therapy I received in the days and weeks following my attempt turned me around and allowed me to let go of seeing this as a suitable escape hatch from pain. Instead, I simply had a few things go my way over the next couple of years, so I kept moving forward.

Until I didn't.

Once I got to college, I began to untether myself from my parents' influence and grieve the trauma I'd survived. That grief turned to rage, instead now it was directed at the ones who had robbed me of the peace and healthy love I was born deserving. I railed at my parents, driving my father out of my life, for good. I wrestled with oppressive guilt over being a disloyal and disrespectful child, yet some force in me had awakened and would not be quieted. Rage became my hero, my spokesperson, my savior. Purging my self-destructive demons required that I deliver their burdens to those responsible for their existence.

I'm not proud of my lack of composure at times during that period of rebellion. Internalized rage following trauma is understandable, yet wrongly placed. Yet, it's quieter. Externalized rage is *loud*. For me, it was wholly unattractive, yet beautiful in its rising. I came to understand that it was inside of me from the start but cloaked in fear of abandonment by my caretaker abusers if I channeled it outward. It protected me at a base level. I had to hold it until I could survive on my own. Then? Take cover.

By the time I reached my sophomore year in college, I'd broken off an engagement to a perfectly loving young man, only to throw my sexuality around to numb out the emptiness I felt. Finally, I had been loved, yet I felt so damaged that I couldn't find a way to maintain the connection. I was barely hanging on mentally, considering the many ways I could take my life while living in the dorms. Pills were harder to come by when I wasn't living with my epileptic and bipolar mom. Pitching myself off the roof would be messy, but probably pretty effective. Decisions, decisions.

Of course my father was still in the picture, extending empty promises about turning around his convict existence, having spent more time in jail than not over the past decade. I was ever hopeful, loyal to the role of his doting, inspirational offspring.

Until I wasn't.

He hadn't been out of prison a day when he relapsed, holing himself up in some meth house, telling me that he was still in jail so he could buy himself some time to be unreachable. When I confronted him about it, every bit of rage that I'd bottled up for those eighteen-plus years came bursting out of me like lava. I couldn't contain it. Frankly, I didn't try.

The survivor in me knew there was a simple choice to make: Him or me.

I chose me.

To say I cut him out of my life that night would be the sanitized version of events. The phone lay in a dozen pieces on the floor as evidence of my fury. This break catapulted me deeper into the therapy I'd just started that week, feeling wholly empowered to begin to live my life on my terms, for me, not for those who had been entrusted with my care. I had healing to do that was long overdue, healing that filled in the cracks of my broken spirit.

Where I'd been existing, I slowly started living. Where I'd been surviving, in time, I began thriving.

I took some hard hits in the years following my emancipation that cold January night.

The powerful shift: Never again did I think of throwing in the towel.

On the contrary, from that night forward, I embraced the rage that set me free and used it as the fire to propel me through the darkness we all must face. I got mad, mad enough to want to get out of the pain I'd been holding onto for too bloody long. When those I loved caused me intentional harm, I spent less time holding myself down in the mud. The rage that once set me free gave way to befriending a stranger named Accountability. The more he showed up, the stronger I became.

Where I had once lived in darkness, I became the light.

Be the light.

~ Using Rage ~

What does all this have to do with my journey…and yours?

Anger…rage even…is a terribly useful thing. I'm not advocating that you wield it irresponsibly and cause injury to passersby. Hurt people hurt people, that's for certain, so take caution. If you've survived a trauma (and statistically most of us *have*), get mad. The message that rage…or any emotion, for that matter…offers us is one of strength, intolerance, and rebellion. When someone hurts us, it SHOULD make us angry! If they do it long and deeply enough, rage is wholly valid. How dare they damage our beauty, tear at our humanity, and place their pain in our flesh? It inspires rightful anger and requires assigned accountability.

I was lucky to find a strong, competent, caring therapist who created depositories for it while I waded through the wreckage of my battered soul. Later, I found companions who helped me channel my anger into compassion, my rage into passion. Compassion and passion became my sword and my pen. It's no small mystery how I write books as effortlessly as I breathe.

Where (and with whom) can you safely and productively process and channel your rage? Find those havens and avenues and use them for your greater good. We all spend some time on the mat. Allow yourself time to rage, heal, and rebuild. Get a therapist. Hire a coach. Join a support group. Journal. Take up boxing. Turn that energy into action toward your recovery. Be gentle with yourself as you allow every emotion to do its job. You are not your trauma. Your rising is what defines you. *Rise.*

~ The Great Divorce ~

If I learned one thing from my healing journey it was this: the ink written on the past is already dry. You cannot alter it. The work required to lighten, to lessen, the pain in our present is to release the pain in our past.

One night, I shared with my best friend, Lisa, a struggle I was having with a deeply *mean* group of women. Being my stalwart nudger, she prompted me to practice the "radical forgiveness" I tout where they were concerned. Sigh. That *I* do what I'm about to tell *you* to do: Feel the angst and actively work to let it pass through me, letting it go.

The timing of her invitation was pretty spot on. I had just explored a similar trail with a client that afternoon, offering her the following mantra to practice when she heard herself recounting old pain stories:

I acknowledge my suffering.

I grieve my suffering.

I release my suffering.

I embrace my healing.

Yeah, all of that. I suppose I could practice what I preach and reap the bounty enjoyed by my clientele, eh?

Can I find compassion for myself, for my caretakers, and our misguided spirits?

I can.

Can I accept us all in our ugly humanity?

Can I move on, leaving our sins in the past where they happened?

Can I experience myself as I am today not as I was so long ago, embracing myself in the present, unburdened by the past?

I can. I can. *I can. I must. I will.*

That's what being a Pain Rebel requires. To leave the past where it happened. To allow it to teach us, strengthen us, but not burden us. Not to confuse the past with the present. Not to allow it to define us perpetually.

That is a violation of pain's purpose.

Radical, repetitive forgiveness and our release of an unchangeable past holds true pain's purpose.

And *that* is the path of the Pain Rebel. That is MY path.

I AM a Pain Rebel. Are you?

When we willingly embrace our beauty and our ugliness, we are invited to the table of acceptance where peace is served.

Repeat after me:

I'm not perfect and I'm working on accepting that/this.

How exactly will we get from judgment to acceptance? Let's break it down into digestible parts, shall we?

~ Intentional Healing ~

Like with everything, to get good outputs we must invest in good inputs. Intention is the very best input there is. When it comes to healing, what does intention look like?

Create space for healing. You've taken the first step by reading this book. Invest in a journal. Take time each day to dig deeper into the activities offered here. Spend time in quiet reflection. Honor silence and the space between where you find yourself and where you want to be.

Sometimes this space is physical. Is there a room in your home that feels heavy and locked in history? Paint it. Reorganize it. Purge it. Do you have keepsakes that bind you to a painful past? Empty that drawer. My yard and tree line had become overgrown, so my boyfriend came by to fix that; he shredded the underbrush and wild, wandering foliage to the ground. He left me with a quiet, uncluttered landscape on which to begin again. Spiritual cleaning can take many, many forms.

Compartmentalize. When it's inconvenient to welcome in the hurt…perhaps you have a big deadline at work or you're on your way to a party you can't get out of…compartmentalize with intention not out of anxiety, fear, and panic. Compartmentalize with intention. That's where your power is.

Vent. Venting moves energy around so you can be intentional. Vent consciously. Do it with purpose to get the ick out of your head and heart but don't get stuck there. Don't be fooled into thinking that venting is the end. You need to take steps to do work of resolving or releasing it before it becomes something ugly inside of you.

In truth, healing occurs in space between relentless pursuit and serene surrender. It is both active and passive, energetic and calm. When you get tired from the fight, rest. When you get tired of waiting, move. Both energies will deliver you recovery.

~ Holding and Withholding ~

Holding rage decreases our power, burdening us with more and ineffectual pain. How? It poisons our spirit and makes us more likely to be the deliverer of injury to others.

Instead of holding the pain, express the anger. Give yourself permission to feel rage. Use the anger to show belief in yourself as a victim yet an intolerance to be a victim anymore. You're worth more than the treatment you received, and the anger communicates that.

But you're holding onto the garbage if you hold the anger and rage and withhold forgiveness. The maddening thing is that those who harmed us are *freer,* yet we are burdened. They've taken their pain and handed it to us, and we've gladly kept holding it. We convince ourselves that holding back forgiveness punishes *them.* In reality, we punish *ourselves*…and others. How?

We think we are protecting ourselves from more hurt but all we're really doing is forcing ourselves to replay our rationale over and over again. We tell ourselves the stories of our pain to remind ourselves why we won't trust/love/risk again. The event is long gone but our memory loop keeps in the present.

We live a life of swimming in the shallow end of the pool.

A man I know had been burned by love. He protected his heart, making it hard for anyone to come inside. He crafted a story that love hurts...and leaves. He was living every day in his broken past. When he found love again, he held her at arms' length. For *years*. When he finally got past his fear, she had been too hurt by his distance to continue. She left. Again, he was burned. Again, he retreated behind his pain. And his story of love equating hurt and abandonment resurfaced. He was in exquisite pain and his only consolation was being right. Like many of us,

He ensured his own heartbreak purely by fearing it.

What's his way out? He needs to complete his grief process. Just because it feels personal when someone leaves us that doesn't make it so. Sometimes people just go. But he's hurting and he can't allow anyone to get close or touch him in his suffering. He's indulging the grief...he's stuck...he's wallowing in it. By doing so, he's ensuring that lovers who are capable and desiring of great love will leave him because he's hidden under a blanket of grief.

I left him, too. After a short time, I found myself so frustrated by his devotion to his old contracts because they were hurting *me*. Luckily, by this point, I'd written my new contracts, so I knew it was time for me to go. I did what I could to guide him toward reckoning with, and releasing, his grief, but he didn't follow me out.

We are inclined to want others to grieve like we do...and in our time...and with our help. That's not how it works. Everyone's grief looks different and not everyone will accept our assistance. It hurts when we intersect with someone else's pain, especially when it hits one of our own raw nerves. We have to ask ourselves if we have patience to watch them clear space, to allow us in...or will we throw up defensive walls or run away screaming? Can you honor their process up close or do you need distance?

Either way, give yourself lots of love. They return us to tears we've yet to shed for other hurts in our own path. We may feel disregarded yet it's often that they don't know how or are not ready to **regard** us. Don't let their muddy hearts dull your sparkle. You don't need to be okay with their (often hurtful) behaviors…and you don't want to jump into the deep end of their head trash. You can clearly state your hurt…that honors it. Their behavior **affects** you, but it's not **about** you…that nuance is very powerful.

Sometimes, like him, we have a part in our own pain. Other times, we don't. We are burned by those who have been burned. We carry the pain they handed to us, yet they remain unaware, unphased, and unaccountable. We might even blame ourselves for the actions of others. Or blame others for our own actions and hurts. Sometimes the person we hurt is our self, sometimes it's others. It's like a game of toxic hot potato: Someone you're near, maybe someone you love, is holding pain. They certainly don't want to feel its burning so they try to hand it to you. You take it and now you feel its burning. If you hang onto it, you'll blister. If you pass it off, then you're responsible for more injury.

What choice do you have?

Ask yourself: Is this my burden to bear? Is there work here for me to do? If so, do the work. If not, choose not to take on a burden that isn't yours. Game over.

~ The "F" Word ~

As I prepared for my TEDx talk in 2018, the consistent message I heard over and over again was how hard forgiveness is. People overwhelmingly felt guilt and shame over not having forgiven someone yet were resolute in staying that course. The reactions were so strong that I actually renamed my talk from "Rage Saved Me, Forgiveness Redeemed Me" to "Secret to Making Life Hurt Less." Everyone was excited to hear the secret, so long as I didn't utter that "f" word. They wanted relief but not *that* way. To be blunt:

We want the outcome without going through the process.

The process I'm advocating requires that we rethink our understanding of forgiveness (and rage) so that we can use both of them to stand in our full Pain Rebel power. Step one: File for divorce. For this divorce you won't need an attorney…just an open mind and willing heart. Get rid of your prior understanding of what forgiveness has meant to you.

"I will not let anyone walk through my mind
with their dirty feet." ~ Gandhi

~ Forgiveness ~

This is my favorite "f" word because it gets far more reactions than "fuck." Forgiveness is such a heavy, controversial term fraught with religious necessity and judgment. When I was sharing the idea for my TEDx talk and I used "forgiveness" in the title, some people came right out and said they'd refuse to watch it if it was going to address *that*. It got me thinking to coin a new term just to reach past other people's defenses.

All kidding aside, forgiveness has been misunderstood, at least the way I define it. Forgiveness doesn't mean that "it" never happened. It doesn't say that you weren't harmed and didn't deserve something far better than you received. It doesn't make you powerless or weak.

In fact, forgiving someone or something is the most powerful thing on the planet.

Forgiveness means that you give up the fantasy that the past can be different. It means letting go of the need to punish someone for your pain. It demands that you see that by **not** offering forgiveness, you're gripping the original injury.

Holding onto the things that have hurt us in the past has us standing in the fire of that pain. We keep those memories close to validate our experience saying, "See how much this must have hurt? See how much I wasn't protected or loved?"

Forgiveness is the water that puts out the fire and stops the burning. It's cleansing, washing away the pain we've been bathing in.

This process refers to you, too. Offer forgiveness to yourself and feel the weight float off your shoulders. Even if you don't feel worthy of forgiveness, consider this: if you don't commit to it, you'll keep dragging around pain and you'll hurt yourself (and others) with it…you'll "bleed on people who didn't cut you" (author unknown). Do you want to keep causing injury? No? Then forgive.

There's a crucial step in forgiveness that a lot of people skip right over, costing them the serenity it can provide: grief. Grief? What does grief have to do with forgiveness? There's a sadness in accepting that the past can't change, that the loss happened and nothing we do in the present or future can amend it. They say that grief is just love with no place to go, so touching our tender wounds bids us to love more. To lean into our grief with compassion and understanding. Love yourself as you release the anger, sadness, disappointment, and attachment to the pain. Allow for that feeling of loss without transforming it into a destructive pattern of thoughts and emotions. In the words of Father Richard Rohr,

"If you do not transform your pain, you will transmit it."

Where do you start? Find the earliest memory of feeling hurt (and perhaps resentful). Recognize that you've had a contract with withholding forgiveness all along, with suffering and punishment. With passing it on to others as sure as you hold it yourself. Burn that mother to the ground, my friend. Let it ***burn***.

~ Using Rage *and* Forgiveness to Heal ~

Trauma creates pain. Internalized pain creates anxiety, depression, and self-defeating patterns. Externalized pain spurs anger, rage, and violence. Each of these manifestations serve a purpose in our recovery from trauma and must be respected and used strategically. Anger creates necessary, but temporary, protection from further pain collection.

Forgiveness is the key out of the pain.

But this isn't your grandmother's forgiveness. Just the word can create a visceral reaction in trauma survivors, so the definition and approach are crucial to its success. Forgiveness, as I use it, is not something you give TO a person, it is something you do ABOUT a person. And, the two-part approach to forgiveness that I practice does something anger (or rage) never could: supports a healthy barrier to future injury AND allows the pain to recede. To bring these points home to the audience, I shared my trauma recovery story which is chronicled in my book, ***Little Landslides*** (2016). Attempting suicide three times by the age of 16, I was a true pain collector and trauma survivor. Raging at, and then forgiving, the man who first beat me bloody when I was 8 weeks old and went on to sexually violate my body as a toddler and beyond was critical in my ability to live an empowered, grateful, abundant life. Yes, I said forgive.

Rage and forgiveness are misunderstood and improperly leveraged techniques in overcoming the pain associated with trauma. With more and more people experiencing trauma (and more and more people committing acts that lead to it), becoming a Pain Rebel offers a way up and out of our pain collecting ways. If we focus on healing pain, we will prevent more of it.

Pain is a natural part of life. The damage comes from holding onto it as a form of protection from new pain. If we see forgiveness as freedom AND protection, we can let go of the pain that creates more pain and distance from others.

When we bring yesterday's hurts forward, we remain victimized, manifesting pain in the future that is rightfully left in the past. We all suffer heartbreaks and broken relationships. I'm not naïve about that and I've welcomed in my fair share of them over the years. One heartbreak in particular brought a new dimension to my perception of "suffering."

Where to start? I fucked up. I know that. I did. I let my own compassion, fear, need for connection, need to be needed…to be someone's hero…obscure my judgment. I couldn't see a path other than the one I followed. I never acted without examination. I was fully conscious for every single, painful step.

What made it so painful? I had a pattern of entering into – and staying in – relationships with those who didn't protect or stand with me when it mattered.

Ohhhhh, old wound right there. How my earliest wounds were a result of no one protecting me from clear and present danger, violation, and abuse. They *loved* me, but they didn't **protect** me.

Because love cannot protect anything. Action protects. Courage protects. Resolve protects. Love, the feeling, just sits there.

Having suffered at the hands of my parents despite their professions of love, I swore to do better with my own children. I needed to do better. They *deserved* better. As with their father, and numerous others, I put my trust in partner after partner who didn't deserve it.

They were weak.

They were scared.

They were broken.

They were traumatized.

They were trying to survive.

They were spiteful.

They were angry.

They were hurt.

They were lost.

They were blind.

They were deaf.

They were crippled.

They felt unworthy.

They felt unlovable

They were not capable of loving me.

When I wrote those words some years ago, I faced a reflection I had long avoided. I saw and accepted those things, that behavior, in them because I saw myself similarly, and I thought I deserved it. My old contracts had never been rewritten and the new ones committed to. The truth: I had *work* to do. What did that tell me?

You return to the wound until you heal it.

That's why I wrote this book: To invite you to return to the wound intentionally instead of poking at it haphazardly. I want this book to be a message of healing, hope, and personal power. To obtain that, guess what's next?

~ Road to Clarity ~

How do you feel and stay safe after you've forgiven someone for harming you?

The answer is as varied as people are, but it comes down to one magical word: Boundaries.

Boundaries are the invisible lines that mark the space between two people. They are the rules about how we allow others to interact with us and what we do in response to them breaking those rules. They separate "my stuff" from "your stuff," allowing us to see what part of our relationship we own. Books can and have been written on this subject alone, so the crucial question is:

How do they fit into forgiveness, feeling safe, and being a Pain Rebel?

They don't just "fit in"…they are ***everything***.

In the past, before we examined and reformed our contracts, we allowed others (or others were allowed) to hurt us and hijack our sense of what was right and wrong. In past incarnations of our relationships, we formed our contracts unconsciously and without intention. Now that we've acquired awareness, there's no going back. We know the cost of absorbing the darkness, of harboring resentment, and perpetuating old patterns. In order to create long-term change, we must shift from anger (or rage) to accountability. There's a huge difference between getting *angry* at people when they cross your boundaries and holding them *accountable*. A POWER difference. Sure, anger feels powerful for a minute, but it doesn't provide what *peaceful* power does.

This power means that you form boundaries and hold people accountable for crossing them. You recognize that you are in control of your thoughts, feelings, and behaviors and that others are in control of theirs. Yet, because we aren't made of stone, we influence one another. Holding this clarity supports you in creating healthy, supportive, and clear relationships. We articulate what we will allow in our lives and what we won't. We negotiate our terms. We know that boundaries are healthy and necessary in relationships. When people are simply careless, or *human*, we hold them accountable for crossing those lines, addressing it clearly and confidently. Not just because it serves us, but because it serves them, too. When people are unhealthy, boundaries empower us to carve intentional distance. In the case of toxic people who refuse to honor our appropriate boundaries, estrangement can be quite intentional.

~ The Beauty of Detachment ~

Detachment, like rage, is a gorgeous element of our humanity.

Detachment doesn't mean being uncaring or unfeeling. On the contrary, detachment is a requirement of deep love. Detachment honors us and our journey, knowing that we if we don't let go, we will be dragged. Let go of what?

So many, many things.

Detachment from outcomes that are not in our control. Detachment from unhealthy patterns and partners. Detachment from our preconceived notions and expectations about what **should** be. Detachment from the thoughts, feelings, and behaviors of others. Detachment from the thoughts, feelings, and behaviors we've indulged that held us prisoner, prisoner to resentment and judgment.

Are you ready to embrace the power of detachment? This exercise is life changing. It comes from the Shamanic tradition and shifts you away from painful ties you've formed. You can use it to detach from another person, even if that other person is a former version of yourself. It's called the:

~ Ropes Exercise ~

Imagine the following: Standing across the person from whom you seek to establish emotional distance. Perhaps they hurt you, left you, deceived you. Somehow, they are taking up space in your heart, head, and it's time for you to separate from them, emotionally. Separating from them will allow new things to move into their space, for you to expend your precious energies on other pursuits and connections. All relationships and connections require energy, an exchange of it. When the relationship is toxic or unhealthy in some way (it might even have been over for years but the energy is still being offered to it through attention and focus), it zaps your energy, leaving you in pain and without the presence required to establish new, healthy connections. As you stand across from them, facing them, just a few feet away, imagine illuminated ropes connecting your chest to theirs. Concentrate on what this connection feels like. It may hurt. You may feel loss, anger, fear, sadness. Linger in this place for a few seconds, clear in the knowledge that this pain is temporary and does not need to remain. Now imagine a gigantic pair of scissors cutting the center of the ropes that connect you to the other person. As you cut, see each side retracting back into you and the person across from you. Take a few deep, cleansing breaths, aware of the energy that has now returned to its rightful place in you. If you feel that old ache, repeat this as you take a few more deep breaths:

"Thank you for this awareness of my pain. You have reminded me to spend time healing myself. Now, I release you."

Feel free to adapt this mantra to one that brings you the most release and relief.

Radical, repetitive forgiveness requires that you return to it again and again when you find yourself emotionally tethered to someone's actions. It stipulates that you release your attachment to what occurred so that you will be free from its harm. Over time, you'll notice that you are finally apathetic when people intentionally hurt you. You *see* what's happening, but you're not *attached* to it emotionally. You choose to love with the knowing that you don't get to choose how that love is received or returned. That, my friends, is true freedom.

Pain Rebels reject…and intentionally release…attachments to painful situations or people.

Pain Rebels move on down the road, in search of their next experience, next love, and next opportunity to fail beautifully and rise majestically.

Key Chapter Concepts

- Rage is beautiful.
- Forgiveness isn't what you thought it was.
- Rage and forgiveness, with boundaries, are game changing.
- Detachment…and the ropes exercise…will free you to become a Pain Rebel.

"Never let someone's ugly mess up your beautiful." ~ *Jennifer Hudson*

12

STORY TIME

"There are parts of you that want the sadness.
Find them out. Ask them why." ~ Yrsa Daley-Ward

We've tackled pain, mindset shifts, and our contracts...both old and new. We've walked through the first four steps of a fruitful change process (awareness, acceptance, analysis, and action). We've attended to the sting that accompanies this entire reckoning process. So, what's next?

Adjustment: What we do once we decide this is the path for us, but we face opposition and resistance? How do we face down the dynamics that threaten to drive us off our chosen road?

When I was writing this book, I became unbelievably waylaid. I'm a healer, a fixer/rescuer-in-recovery! I want to HELP. I want to deliver ease and hope.

Unlike any other book, I avoided writing **Pain Rebel** like the plague. I was wholly – and painfully (hah!) – stuck. I could have had it done months before my car accident (that derailed me more)...but I ran from it. I rebelled against the rebel? Lol. No. That's not it at all. It's because I'm offering up a solution for what's holding us back....and I myself am *tethered*.

I had been plagued by this desperate sensation that lurks just behind my consciousness. As I made my way through even the most mundane daily tasks, I was overwhelmed by a profound sadness, a powerful invitation to fall into an endless stream of tears. Sometimes I'd pause, welcoming them in, but they never came. There was a wall of some sort holding them back.

But, the darkness behind the veil remained. I carried it with me every day. It wasn't the paralyzing, disabling sadness I'd felt in the past, but it was thick, nevertheless, and further from my grasp. What in the hell was it?

~ My Inner Critic ~

Many of us are plagued by an inner critic, me included. In my case, my Inner Critic takes the form of an Inner Chatterer; she's non-freaking-stop! I kid you not; this voice fills every gap like a nosy, nit-picking, hyper-active, never-been-married-or-engaged aunt who you can't shake to save your life at the family reunion. She. Never. Shuts. Up.

Oh, I've tried calming her down, I have. With years and years of mindfulness practice, she's tempered a bit. A teensy, weensy little bit. Yet, her obtrusive-ness is unparalleled.

You'd think that writing would be effortless for me; if my mind is full of persistent chatter then it follows that I could fill up endless file cabinets with my thoughts, right? Well, yes, that's technically correct. The problem with this *particular* book is that its essence is the backbone of Ms. Inner Chatterer herself: Suffering. And not just your run-of-the-mill suffering. No, no. This unique brand of suffering is rooted in my life's mission: to save other people *from* it.

Pain Rebel

I want to offer the key to break you out of the prison of your pain. I want to stop your suffering and my Inner Chatterer is terrified I'll fail.

You see, I grew up in the shadow of other people's pain; their suffering became my own. *Their* anger became *my* scars. *Their* sadness became *my* fear. *Their* emptiness became *my* depression.

I hurt because *they* hurt. If only I could find a way to spare *them,* I could spare *myself.* If I could get *them* to stop hurting, *I* could stop hurting.

Old ghosts die hard. I wasn't conscious of this inner torment until my fingers were magnetically repelled from my keyboard. I knew I wanted to write a book about re-crafting your relationship to pain so you could make life hurt less. What I didn't know was that the little girl in me was in charge of the flow of my words.

That little girl was setting up this book to be the realization of that mission. She was terrified that she would fail to save others in the way she failed to save her parents.

Yeah, just *that.*

I was immobilized. Every time I contemplated working on this book I got so overwhelmed by anticipatory guilt and shame, rooted in the fear that I will fail you, my readers; that I'll fall short of saving you from life's innate suffering.

Because I will. I *will* fail in my auspicious mission.

This book…or me in real life…cannot save you from pain.

Pain is, in fact, inevitable. Because it is the cost of love. Of caring about anything. If you love, you *will* hurt. Nothing and no one can save you from that. C'mon, that's why they call them growing *pains* not growing *pleasures.*

How We Take Our POWER Back

So, what can *you* do?

Rewrite the story.

~ Contracts = Narrative ~

I'm no mathematician but I'm somewhat familiar with the transitive property: If $A=B$ and $B=C$ then $A=C$.

Our contracts create our perceptions. Rewriting our contracts shifts our self-perception. Our self-perception shifts our perception of others. Together, these shift our worldview. Therefore, our contracts equal our narrative.

Take for instance, contracts that paint us as victim. Real victims don't possess much, if any, power. When people feel like victims (or powerless), they are more likely to hand over any power they *do* have.

Let's get one thing straight: Being victimized is an event or series of events; living as a victim is a story.

The victim-storied don't *believe* they have agency. The victim-storied don't like confrontation because they might get called out on their own narrative and held accountable. We've all been stuck in the swirl of a victim story, haven't we? And we convince ourselves and others of the version we are telling. Like any good salesperson,

We can sell any story we tell.

The more we tell the story, the more we believe it. The more people we tell the story to, the more complicated the web becomes when we want to create a new narrative. The good news is that change begins within us, at a cellular level. Adopting a new narrative interrupts the neuropathways of a victim story. This doesn't happen overnight, mind you. We work and we make progress toward awareness versus reactivity by getting consumed by our story about the pain. There are no magic wands or pixie dust. Don't be mesmerized by the charm of being Cinderella: Rescue your damn self.

~ Noticing ~

It's simple. Notice.

Notice yourself being harsh with yourself. Notice yourself being harsh with others. Notice yourself winning small victories. Notice your kindness toward others. Do you find yourself being kinder to your friends than you are to yourself? Think of what you said to your very best friend the last time he or she was struggling. How encouraging were you? Could you see what they couldn't see? Were you able to find their grace and beauty when they felt low? Now, change the pronouns in what you said from "you" to "I/me." Turn that compassion and congratulation inward. Maybe you wrote a new contract about being gentler with others? The next time you start browbeating someone else (even if only in your mind), flip those pronouns. If those judgments were coming at you, what compassion would you want extended to you? Extend it to them.

Noticing exposes choice, therefore noticing is power.

Remember: We drown not by falling in the water, but by staying submerged in it. Float.

~ Cognitive Distortions ~

Cognitive distortions commandeer our thinking. To take our power back, we have to see that our thoughts do not need to be entertained or indulged. That they can simply be thoughts without incident. If the thought seems negative or limiting, we can challenge it and ask, "does this thought serve my greater good?" If it doesn't, we can use the simplest, yet most effective, tool ever:

The word "**or**."

What does "or" do? It instills flexibility in our thinking. It shows us that we aren't wedded to our thoughts. That we know that other thoughts might have value. Just like shame grows in the shadows, pain deepens in certainty. Why? Because our cognitive distortions go unchallenged. When our thinking is distorted, we are apt to make decisions and indulge feelings that create more unrest.

Want to stop a negative thought train? First you have to understand how your thinking works in the first place.

You can't NOT think about something. Don't believe me?

Don't think about a warm piece of pizza. No, don't. Don't think about the pizza. The cheese dripping from the edges, sauce poking out through the gaps. Stop thinking about it. It's going to clog your arteries and leave you with indigestion. Don't do it. Don't think about a warm piece of pizza.

Betcha you've already added all the toppings.

You're not failing when you fixate on a thought, particularly one that's been tangled in your mind for years (or one about a delectable dinner item!). Instead you have to replace a thought with another (hopefully, desirable) thought or with intentional quiet (as in meditation).

Think about a shiny, crisp, sweet apple. How it feels in your hand and as it touches your lips right before you take a delicious bite out of it. How the juice will taste as you snap a piece off between your teeth. Think about how both your hunger and thirst will be quenched by this satisfying treat.

You've likely forgotten all about the pizza.

Thought replacement works in all sorts of applications. I know it's said that men have a one-track mind, but the truth is each of us only have one track we can fully occupy at a time. To be the master of your thoughts, you must see that you choose:

Which thoughts to entertain,

Which thoughts to replace, and,

How seriously to take them.

If you have a thought that isn't serving you but you're not replacing it, you still get to decide how seriously to take them. Will you hop on the runaway thought train till you do something a future you would regret, *or* will you see it as a fleeting thought and just let it go? Negative thoughts don't have to create unrest within you; they're simply a signal to zero in on thought mastery.

Speaking of unrest, fear is one of the most misused results of cognitive distortions. How? When we fear something, in essence we are saying we want the opposite. For instance, suppose you are afraid of getting fired. Focusing on something you don't want doesn't spur action. Better tactic: Focus on where you want to go. What we *want* is to keep our job (or quit on our own terms, perhaps!). **Want** inspires action and solidifies our power position. When we want something, we work toward it. When we focus on our fear, the opposite happens. Fear saps our power and has no place for intention and action. We are caught in a powerless rut, but empowerment is just a thought shift away.

Want less pain? Become a thought shifter by being more flexible in your thinking.

~ The Three Cs ~

As much as flexibility is leverage in empowerment, the true superpowers are the twins: **consideration** and **curiosity**. Their nemesis? **Certainty**.

How We Take Our POWER Back

Our inclination is to make statements of certainty. We know what we know, right? Often, we take a stand that we not only know what we are thinking and doing, but also everyone else on the planet. There's a problem? We know why it happened and who's at fault. They make us feel in control of what is and what can be. We flood our brains with statements of certainty, convincing ourselves of the story we are telling. Story? Yes, story. Because rarely are statements of certainty 100% certain. But not according to *our* story. If we have one fixated story, we limit our choices as to how to see the situation and possible responses.

Want to expand your choices? When you feel drawn into a conversation, a decision, or an action, take a position of **consideration** instead. Consider your position. Consider your impulses. Consider your feelings. Consider your options. Don't get sucked into a statement of certainty. Use your elevated awareness to consider your choices.

Embrace **curiosity**. Connected to a position of consideration, a curiosity stance embraces the unknown. Curiosity is how we boost our awareness, increase our choice, and maximize our power. As such, it requires a degree of confidence and comfort in uncertainty. That's where our power is. We invest in finding **clarity**, in discovering various perspectives, in challenging our assumptions. Assumptions are both feeble and ineffective. Our typical quest for **conformity** demands that life conform to our preconceived notions and old tapes about the way things are and *should* be. Instead, as a leader, as a regular old person, as a Pain Rebel, we must have informed intention. We must know *what* we are committing to before we commit. We must be curious, inquisitive. When we drop our attachment to how things *should* be, we can get busy on how we *want* them to be. When someone behaves badly toward us, we don't get stuck in the script of "I should be mad" or "I should give them a piece of my mind." Sure, a witty (or stinging) retort feels powerful. Do you know what feels more powerful?

Being fully in control of yourself. Completely intentional in all you say and do.

Speaking of feeling powerful, let's talk about two words and five letters that'll change your life.

~ The Two Truths ~

It truly is easier to hold just one truth. Certainty feels safe. We crave safety. Our monkey brains demand it. The truth is there are so many slices, so many aspects, of truth. The harder you tighten around one, the harder it is to see our choices, power, and path toward peace.

Two of the shortest and simplest words in the English language are also the most transformational. Both of them shift our devotion to our one, limiting, often flawed truth. The first is "and," the second is "or."

How many times have you been bitching about a certain person and assigned a motive to why they were doing a certain thing? Plenty, am I right? Me, too. We do it all the time. We want to understand things and control the narrative so we can decide how justified we are to respond in a certain way. I see this all the time in office dramas. A co-worker or manager gets painted in a certain light without ever considering the plethora of possible other frames on a situation, without considering that person's unique perspective.

Or, alongside **and**, changes all of that.

How does it work? When we catch ourselves telling the story as to why they're doing the thing, simply follow it with "or" and finish that prompt once or twice or three times. That's it? Yup. That's it. I told you it was simple but profound. You're allowing yourself to consider another possible reality, one that might spur your curiosity to investigate its merit. Maybe you'll ask some questions to get to the bottom of it? Maybe you'll be curious more than certain the next time you face a similar challenge? If so, you'll increase your possible responses and are far less likely to get worked up. Calmness serves you, my friend, and everyone around you.

In essence, using **or** minimizes our need to be right, an instinct that wastes our precious energy proving others wrong. The silver lining is that when we let go of our certainty, we can actually **be** right more often. Funny irony, huh?

What about **and**? This brings me back to a concept I introduced in my third book, a book about the change process: ***Stuck U.*** Spectrum surfing spoke to how our qualities are not an either/or situation: They are held on a spectrum.

People can be both responsible and irresponsible; kind and mean; tender and harsh. Even if this isn't true for their overall character, it is for their behavior.

I don't know about you, but I know I'm not 100% anything all of the time. I can be both selfish and giving in the very same breath. Take a simple thing like running as a hobby. The runner could be seen as selfish for all the time they spend away from family out hitting the pavement. At the same time, they could be viewed as giving for both preserving their health and longevity but also for raising funds for charity in their benefit races. Often, when we get into conflicts, we jump to one end of the spectrum in levying our judgment (inwardly or outwardly). We think people need to be "this" ***or*** "that."

We fall into an age-old trap: It is far easier to judge someone than to seek to understand them.

Sometimes the truth is quite intricate. For those of you who've read my fifth book and autobiography, ***Little Landslides***, you might recall the photo I have on the back cover. For those of you who haven't, it's tough to do justice in a written description but it's a photo of me as a toddler with my dad and a lion. Yes, a full-grown male lion. I've had this photo in a frame since I was a very young child, a photo I saw daily throughout my childhood, in tandem with his abuse. Why do I still display it? Because Pain Rebels hold inconvenient, coexisting truths like love AND hate. Misery AND joy. Laughter AND tears. It's often not one or the other, it's both.

And also applies to seeing things differently from another person. The example I like to use is being told we are beautiful, yet we don't believe it. We feel unworthy of adoration, so the compliment falls on deaf ears. Instead of rejecting that truth as falsehood, suspend certainty. Leave open the possibility that it could hold truth. That you could be *seen* as beautiful AND *feel* ugly. That both can coexist. Seeing our "and"-ness changes everything.

In essence, using **and** helps us hold the good and the bad simultaneously, the ugliness of evil alongside the beauty of goodness. Positioned this way, we lessen the assignment of blame and expand our willingness to come from forgiveness and love with everyone we meet. It's a game changer.

Both words (and/or) encourage us to appreciate multiple viewpoints and aspects of the world around us. When we don't use them consciously, we are more apt to create a world of "us vs. them," blaming others for our lot in life. This busts relationships apart, creating opposing sides that devolve into warring factions. **Or,** alongside **and**, breaks the battle lines and inhibits resentment.

Remember the pins near the Pain Rebel on the cover? These words repel them. Buh-bye. Not *this* Pain Rebel. Not today.

~ Power Grid: Awareness and Acceptance ~

"But, Dr. B, I've been going to therapy and following a self-help journey for decades and I think I know every nook and cranny of my psyche and all the whys for the things I do and the choices I'm making and I'm still in pain. What gives?"

I'm so flipping glad you asked!

You, like a disproportionate section of the population, missed a critical element in maximizing your full power deployment: Acceptance.

Terribly often I see people who have grown dramatically in awareness yet are downright miserable and feel a fraction of the power available for their use.

As you age, develop, and grow in awareness, you also rise in power (remember awareness equals choice equals power). The next influential step is acceptance. What do I mean by "acceptance?"

Accepting responsibility to fix something or shut up about it. Accept it or change it; there is no other sane option.

For example: You come downstairs every morning to find unwashed dishes in the sink. This is a pet peeve of yours, so you start each day off in a sour mood. You're stompy and angry and it affects how you feel for the rest of the day. How do you arrive at a power position? First consider this chart.

Below are the quadrants listed from low to high desirability.

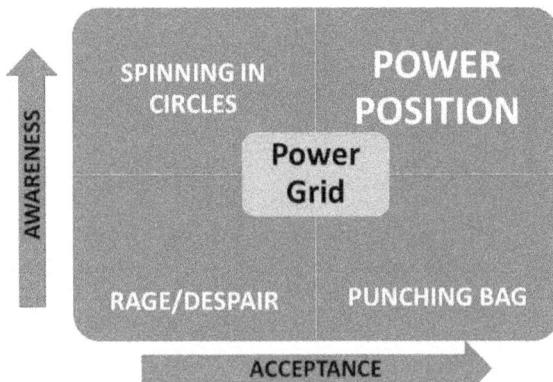

Rage/Despair: Low Awareness plus Low Acceptance

Punching Bag: Low Awareness plus High Acceptance

Spinning in Circles: High Awareness plus Low Acceptance

Power Position: High Awareness plus High Acceptance

Let's get back to the dirty dishes.

What is a power position response? First, you are aware of your frustration. Next, you accept responsibility to either change the situation or accept it as it is. As a result, you consider your options for changing it. Maybe you'll have a family meeting. Perhaps you'll speak with each person one by one. Or instead, you'll write a cute note on the counter before you go to bed with your request. If all of these fail, or you deploy none of them, you simply accept there being dishes in the sink. Your family is happy and healthy, you are safe and satisfied; maybe the dishes are just the price you pay for the rest of your blessings and you're cool with that.

"I follow four dictates: Face it, accept it, deal with it,
then let it go." ~ Master Sheng Yen

~ Acceptance and Change ~

If I haven't made this clear before, thoughts are not the enemy. They are information that we have a certain narrative that might benefit from being amended. Feelings are not the enemy. Feelings alert us when we feel discomfort. How you interpret them is your second line of defense when your thoughts lead you astray.

How We Take Our POWER Back

What you're thinking is not who you are, it's just your programming. What you're feeling is not who you are, it's a direct consequence of your programming.

When we move to action, things get more complicated. In the words of Will Durant (not Aristotle who often gets credit), "You are what you repeatedly do." The way to change who you are is to break your patterns. How do you do that?

Know that whatever is happening is not who you are. You can choose what you're doing and influence what is happening. You have choice and choice equals power. Ask yourself: How is this serving my greater good? What actions CAN I take to enhance my greater good?

How does acceptance fit into this?

It's all up to you now. You got here predictably, through a series of circumstances marked by choices; choices in perception, feeling, and behavior. The only way you'll get out is the same way—by your own volition.

As I cover in much more detail in my book, **Stuck U.**, there are two parts to acceptance: 1) accepting how you got to this point; and, 2) accepting that you want change and are responsible for that change. Some believe the illusion that acceptance means relinquishing your power when, in fact, it delivers an abundance of it. Acceptance puts you in charge of how you expend your precious energy, how you move toward change.

Taking back your power presents challenges: first and foremost? Ownership and accountability. If you accept things as you find them, you'll be forced to give up the blame game. There's no one to point a finger at anymore when you're the one in charge of your trajectory. Sure, others may have created some crappy conditions, but how you see them and what you do in response to them is all on you.

~ Director ~

My younger daughter and I watch a lot of movies together, once cycling through the entire Marvel™ Universe in a couple of weeks. We'll often yell at the screen when one of the characters is doing something perilous…or just stupid…but they don't listen. Like when you're watching a horror flick and you're befuddled that they don't sense the killer approaching…I mean, can't they HEAR the MUSIC? From the comfort of your couch, you're hollering your impotent warnings at a flatscreen.

Am I the only one who holds two-sided conversations with people who aren't there, rehearsing what I'll say AND what they'll say? I can entertain myself for hours with these imaginary scenarios. You, too, huh? The coolest thing is that if I don't like one undeniably sassy comeback I deliver, then I just rewind my imagination and redo it. "CUT!" Of course, either way, the other person always falls short, so I win the verbal battle. Woohoo! Yeah, but not so much…since they WEREN'T EVEN THERE! It happened only in my mind which is why it went so perfectly.

Back to my daughter and me and our movie marathon…

Even as a little girl, when we were watching any old thing on the screen, she'd ask me, "Mommy, WHY are they doing that?!?!" My response? "Because the director told them to."

The same thing happens on *our* life's stage:

We wait for others in our lives to respond to the director's cue and follow the (*our*) script. But they don't. They fail us. Because (wait for it….)

They have a DIFFERENT *SCRIPT*.

They have a DIFFERENT *DIRECTOR*.

So, what do you do? Well, first off, recognize that you're following different scripts and directors. Then, share your script. Talk about what you were expecting to happen. Dig deeper and tell the person what you need and want. Have a meaningful, vulnerable conversation and negotiate a new script. And never again assume that you share a story with anyone.

~ Keep the Garbage Out ~

You're probably thinking: "Please tell me you have tips on how to live with fewer crappy conditions and relationships in the first place!"

Sure do! Repeat after me:

I live in calm. The anxiety of others lives in others. Their behavior is an indication of the contracts they're abiding by. I purposefully choose...and abide by...my own contracts.

The beauty industry advises us on how to stave off visible signs of aging: cleanse, exfoliate, moisturize. The same holds true for our hearts and minds. To feel vibrant and young, we are called to cleanse our thinking and our patterns of behavior; to shed the layers of hurt that are distracting and stressing us out; to nourish ourselves with kind and supportive treatment so we can be our best possible selves. The risk, of course, when we shed those layers and become softer and more supple, is that we *feel* more readily. This can seem risky in an often unkind world. Ask yourself, though, what is better? Leathery and cynical or soft and hopeful.

I'll choose the latter seven days out of seven.

When we are soft and hopeful, we can attract broken souls because they sense our passionate compassion. Like a car wreck, we don't look away, we stop to help. Most people keep driving. Maybe your new, healthy path is to *see* them but not become *absorbed* by them.

And live by example. You can offer help, but you cannot save them from themselves. My dad used to say, "You can't save anyone who doesn't want your help." The challenge is to distinguish those who desire your help from those who don't. Is saving people how you define love? Does that love include your martyrdom? If so, redefine it. Establish boundaries that protect your strength and joy. Fill your tank so that you have enough left over to help. What does that sound like?

"I love you. I want you to feel better. What can you do to help yourself? I want to help you and I know that the only way I can support you is if I'm strong. I get weak when I try to help too much."

How can you keep garbage out? By saying, reading, and living intentionally by your new contracts, practicing good self-care, and taking time to grieve your old contracts. You invested a chunk of your life believing in and living by those agreements and it cost you. As they say in sports circles: the best defense is a good offense. Don't wait for energy vampires to bite before you respond with that mantra. Are you conscious of what's going on? Do you know what you deserve?

"Be the love you never received." ~ Rune Lazuli

~ Most Improv-ed ~

The path to being a Pain Rebel, isn't a short, straight one. Healing never comes all at once. It takes time. Growth isn't linear; it's more like the cha-cha. Two steps forward, one step back…if you're lucky. Progress simply means that we learn more each time we return to a familiar situation. We know the questions to ask and things to say to move us away from that place more quickly and with less fallout. Lessons are simply stories in your hero journey.

What are these lessons you're learning? Reflect on them. Journal about them. Challenge them to ensure they fit with your **new** contracts not your **old** contracts. Are you getting to the lessons quicker? Are you steeping in the ick for less time? You know you've begun to transform your relationship with pain when you can find progress in:

How deeply it hurts, and
How long it stays.

Celebrate the baby steps. Look at the in-the-moment progress. Have you improved? Do you react (sign of old contracts putting you on autopilot) less and respond (thoughtful, intentional, new-contract-based) more? I like to think of improved as improv-ed. With improv, you're fully in the moment, thinking on your feet but drawing on your training and wealth of creativity and choice. When you know you've improved is when your improv game is on point. You see. You choose. You respond. You learn. You move on.

Change isn't effortless, but it comes if we seek it.

~ Great & Powerful Pause ~

Remember our Pain Rebel mantra?

Awareness equals choice and choice equals power.

Awareness and choice are the hallmarks of a Pain Rebel. All of your power is anchored in awareness because it reveals choice. What is the fastest way to develop more awareness? Well, since lacking awareness relies on operating on autopilot and cramming our lives with busy work and distractions in a race to nowhere…

Slow the fuck down.

Think about the last time you drove to the grocery store. When you went through an intersection on your way, did you fly through it or look around as you passed? The faster you went the harder it was to see if another vehicle or pedestrian (or errant, suicidal squirrel) was in your way, right? If you couldn't see them coming, you couldn't defensively maneuver your way out of danger, could you? The same holds true for us traveling down the road of life: If we are consumed by racing to our next destination (conversation, meeting, to-do list item), we won't notice how many choices are available to us as to how to respond to any given situation. Autopilot doesn't see choice. Autopilot sees efficiency as success. Autopilot counts on past patterns to control (and therefore, limit) responses.

Pain Rebels are greedy for *lots* of choice.

Why? Because Pain Rebels like to have lots of personal power. But with great power comes great responsibility (gotta love Stan Lee!). My mom was right when she told me:

The one with more awareness has more responsibility.

It's the reason why we have a designated driver: The sober person can see what the drinker can't see, so they are in charge.

The good news in raising consciousness is that higher consciousness translates into greater success and abundance. Why? You can see what others can't see. Think of an Easter egg hunt. If you're in the moment, scanning the environment, you're more likely to fill your basket. It works the same way with life: when you want more out of life, tune into it. Notice. Then catch yourself before you act. Don't get caught in judgment, just pause and see what you see. Increasing the space between **what you notice** and **what you _do_ about what you notice** inserts **choice**. And what does that lead to? Power.

**Pain Rebels increase the space between moments
to increase their power.**

Power doesn't mean that things won't challenge and upset us. Power means that we will consciously decide how to respond to those things. Our humanity makes us vulnerable, but it also enables us to live life fiercely, validating and protecting ourselves with the power of choice. When pain comes, we can choose to let it leave.

One of our greatest pains as a collective is anxiety. Our anxiety multiplies the more we race our way through life. Exercising our powerful pause opens the door to holding our anxiety in a warm and welcoming place instead of trying to bury or deny it. We can ask ourselves what we need to find our way out of our frenetic thinking. We can allow thoughts to come and go without judgment. We can consciously decide what to do next instead of being locked in frenzied programming. In pausing to bear our feelings, we see pain's splendor.

Can pain be an awakening to places you need to heal and grow? Absolutely. If you feel lost, know that being lost is not a permanent state. If you feel anxious, you're probably spinning in circles and not getting anywhere. Pause. Breathe. Taking an intentional pause in the face of stress and strife isn't anything like spinning. A pause requires emotional distance and intellectual perspective. A pause is a power position. If you feel like you're hanging by a thread, increase its thickness. Challenge your thinking. Ask yourself: What thoughts am I holding that might be contributing to my current experience? Consider your options. Choose your next right step. The meaning of life is to learn and grow so embrace the tough moments.

"It was her habit to build laughter
out of inadequate materials." ~ John Steinbeck

~ Emotional Barometer ~

If you're starving, you're unlikely to craft an intricate meal; instead, you'll raid the pantry and stuff your face with a bag of potato chips. Like hunger, anger seeks immediate relief. We take shortcuts to get that relief and neglect to consider (let alone act on) our full menu of options. That's why they speak of being "blinded by anger" because we can't see what's really important to us, what we deeply value.

For example, suppose we are stuck in old contracts, contracts that tell us things like, "when someone – anyone – disrespects you it's your job to knock them down a few pegs and punish them for their misbehavior." Enter: your friend who doesn't show up for your lunch date that's been planned for weeks.

What do you do?

Our old contracts would advise that we call to yell at her and maybe return the favor the next time she calls to make plans. Or shut her out completely and write her off as our friend. That'll teach her.

If we could insert a pause to consider what we actually wanted, we could take intentional steps to get there. What might we want in the end? Maybe it's to preserve and improve the relationship? We could stand in integrity by acting in consistency with our true desires. What might those be?

Maybe it's embodying peace and compassion instead of anger and judgment.

If we slowed our roll, we could consider our new contracts and choose to follow them. What might our new contracts tell us? Maybe it's to ask for an explanation, calmly communicate our disappointment, and set our boundaries clearly with this friend (that you require a call if they aren't dying or detained, for example). Maybe we discover that there is a very valid reason behind her tardiness.

Unfortunately, when you feel harmed, your ego gets in the way. Your ego wants to protect and defend you, so it's a shitty gatekeeper for your growth. Your ego can't decide what's useful or right or fair if you want to grow. When information and experience get stuck at the ego level, growth is thwarted. Ego is all about survival.

How We Take Our POWER Back

The biggest and deepest regrets I have were from hurts I inflicted when I operated on emotion, reaction, ego, and pride. We do that when we fail to pause, to consider, to choose with intention a new path. Our new path is comprised of new contracts. That path doesn't just show up...it has to be chosen over and over again. If we don't choose it consciously, our old contracts will continue to drive our unconscious patterning.

My old contracts were ripe with dysfunction. Growing up, I don't recall feeling calm, ever. The overall tempo was anxiety-ridden, and there was more drama than a soap opera. My (older) sister was troubled and loud, demanding more than her share of attention. I grew up in the shadow of her unrest. Our relationship had warmer and cooler times in our adulthood, but my heightened awareness of her instability kept me from ever feeling close to or trusting of her.

When our mother suddenly died a number of years ago, we stood on a razor's edge. Predictably, she took up all the space in the room as we grieved our mom's passing and addressed the messy estate process. Again and again, I felt myself drawn into the drama that marked my early years. I felt the rage of having been dominated and minimized over and over. The estate entered probate and to say it was convoluted and bursting with personal issues is an understatement. Our narratives couldn't have been more different; each of us being painted as the villain. To avoid the estate being judged bankrupt, we ended up in mediation.

As I sat in a sterile office just outside of Boston, awaiting my meeting with a retired judge who would determine our fates, I wrote the following:

I am peace
I am beauty
I am love
I am calm
I am truth
I am just

190

Pain Rebel

Therefore,

I hold peace
I hold beauty
I hold love
I hold calm
I hold truth
I hold justice

I surrender.
There is no fight in me. The fight exists in resistance.
I release resistance. I hold only light.
I welcome endings and new beginnings.

Suffice it to say, this meeting went differently. I *was* different. I knew that she was in pain. I was convinced that her pain and her patterns had her stuck. I acknowledged that regardless of my efforts, it was likely that I wouldn't receive fair treatment. From that place of calm acceptance, I didn't react. I didn't let my emotions cloud my intention to hold to those words no matter what bait was thrown my way. I put my ego needs down and stayed anchored in my pause. When her lawyers advocated for an unfair result, I saw it for what it was: A tactic.

Pain Rebels don't react to tactics. We are thoughtful in our responses, so I was. I clarified. I pointed out their delirium. But I kept my composure. When I left the office empty handed, I was at peace. I had done nothing to feel guilty or embarrassed about. I saw the craziness of the interaction, but I didn't take on any of its toxicity.

Sure, I would have been justified in yelling at her attorneys and making a scene. I had before. She did then. But if I did, I'd have a burden to take home with me. I wanted freedom more than anything. Freedom that came from having integrity; integrity because I held firm to my values and intentions without letting the world sway me.

~ Concluding Thoughts ~

This chapter really packed a powerful punch of critical concepts and approaches! I think the box below does a better job than some repetitive paragraph ever could, so let's get to it!

Key Chapter Concepts

- Our inner critic can derail us.
- Our contracts collectively form our narrative.
- Noticing our thoughts creates power through choice.
- Cognitive distortions are deepened by certainty and foiled by consideration and curiosity.
- Using two words (and, or) increases consideration and curiosity.
- The Power Grid showcases the relationship between awareness and acceptance.
- Everyone is following a different script and director.
- Improvement is demonstrated by how deeply things hurt and how long the feeling lasts.
- Pauses create power.

"A person grows in beauty whenever they move away from what harms them and into their power." ~ Yung Pueblo

13

CONCLUDING THOUGHTS

"You didn't come this far to only come this far." ~ Mick Kremling

This was anything but a passive voyage. I challenged you. I questioned you. I poked at the places you've kept hidden. I pushed you to get honest with yourself about how your relationship to pain is causing you more. How living in your story is preventing you from inhabiting a better one.

I know this isn't easy. But look: You're already IN. You read this book. You've already intervened upon your mindset and entertained new tactics for getting your needs met. What's next? Keeping your promise to yourself. It requires a relentless pursuit of joy and resilience, something you were born for. Imagine if more of us joined together on this trek? How different would the world be? Truth be told, that's my true, sinister plan (muahaha!). I want to encourage individual, transformational change that inspires a social movement, a change that will lessen our pain, trauma, and unhappiness. I want joy. Elation. I want bliss.

How We Take Our POWER Back

In order to do that, I've needed to be the frightening, revealing dressing-room mirror that wakes you up to what our ugly really looks like under those fluorescent lights.

Don't worry if you're feeling like a work in progress...we all are. Just because you aren't at the finish line...whatever that entails...doesn't mean you haven't made progress.

Suppose your weight got out of control and you tipped the scales at 500 pounds. You were miserable, exhausted, hopeless, and isolated. Your awareness of the cost of these extra pounds led to your acceptance of your situation. You dove head-first into analysis followed by action. You changed your eating patterns, gradually incorporated exercise into your daily routine, and sometime later, found yourself weighing 250 pounds. You lost half your body weight! You were no longer breathless walking up a flight of stairs, your blood pressure plummeted, cholesterol leveled out, and you began shopping in regular clothing stores.

Can you hear the "but" coming?

BUT, you're not at your target body size. You have a while to go before you reach a healthy weight. You've been taking action but there are so many days you wake up and feel like a failure. You want to be at the finish line but you're not. You're still on the track and it's taking a short infinity to reach your destination.

In the adjustment phase, the place you find yourself when you've been at this Pain Rebel thing for a while, I invite you to adjust your mindset. To check your perceptions. To evaluate the reality of your path to this point. We have an annoying tendency to judge our success from starting point to ending point with little regard for the journey itself. You've lost 250 pounds! That's amazing! Sure, you're not done yet, but attend to how different you feel, how much of an impact your progress has had on every layer of your existence. You've likely added years to your life already! Yeah, you've got a ways to go, but I assure you that you'll get there a whole lot faster, happier, and easier if you celebrate your progress on the path. If you take note of where you **were** versus ruminating on where you're **not yet**. You're not done yet. Keep going. Adjust your attitude, buckle down on your passion-oriented goal, and continue to take the next, right action.

Having spent countless hours steeped in addiction recovery treatment and literature, the "one day a time" mantra is burned in my hippocampus. Pain Rebels concede that we can only live today *in* today. To live heroically and passionately, we must take radical, repeated action toward recovery. Simultaneously, we prepare for slippage, admitting our humanness. We are patient with our transformation, grateful for every step out of our past suffering.

Pain Rebels also hold clear boundaries and acknowledge where our power ends: at the edges of ourselves. We don't control the actions and responses of others. If you picked up and devoured this book thinking that it was going to provide the potion to change someone in your life, you've wasted your time. (Well, not really since you picked up some useful stuff for **you**.) I know you want to help. I know you think your path out of pain is connected to theirs, but that's only a part of the story. Sure, sprinkling some pixie dust would provide the fast-track to your healing, but it's not the way of the Pain Rebel. You do the work for *you*. You don't judge the effectiveness of your actions against the reactions of others. You don't control **them**. You control **you**.

~ Summing Things Up ~

I close any seminar or course I teach with the following question: What's your big takeaway? Of course, I hope they are taking away a laundry list of insights, but there's no time for all that at the end of a presentation.

You, on the other hand, have plenty of time to reflect. What did you learn? Where do you go from here? Who can support the changes you're making?

How We Take Our POWER Back

No one travels this passage alone. Pain Rebels enlist the help of others. One of my boyfriend's favorite quotes is, "If you want to know who you'll become, look at your friends and there's your answer." Who are you surrounding yourself with? Are you spending time with those who are tied to their old contracts? Or are you linked to people who are on a path of growth who will encourage you to join them? Do you see guides in your life? Remember, you can't change the people around you, but you can change the people around you (you might need to say that a few times before the meaning reveals itself).

This doesn't mean that everyone in your life has to be in front of you on the path; part of your job as a Pain Rebel is to look through the door you just walked through and reach back to take someone else's hand. Offer this new mindset to others in your life and along your journey who are pain collectors. Offer them compassion and guidance. Speak to them of this new way you've discovered that has made all the difference.

Speak your truth, resist the pull to go back to seeing pain as anything other than information, a temporary signal to pay attention and attend to a wound…one in the present and some in the past.

If you find yourself discouraged, and things look grim, search for three beautiful things in your world. If you can't find them no matter how hard you try, BE them. BE the beauty you seek.

Speaking of beautiful, turn the page and soak in the Pain Rebel Creed. This is your talisman, your guide, your reinforcement to make choices every day consistent with your truest, deepest, most glorious potential.

You deserve nothing less.

"When I was a boy and I would see scary things in the news,
my mother would say to me, 'Look for the helpers.
You will always find people who are helping.'" ~ *Fred Rogers*

PAIN REBEL CREED

I am a Pain Rebel.

I choose to own my thoughts, feelings, and behaviors because I know that they hold my joy and embody my gratitude.

I acknowledge that awareness equals choice and choice equals power. I commit to unearthing my unconscious drives and contracts so that I can choose deliberately and flourish in my personal, peaceful power.

I invest in myself and my bountiful potential by rewriting my contracts and devoting my energy to healthy new contracts.

I acknowledge that my old contracts helped me to survive; I honor my path and let go of shame for the pain I held before I knew more.

I deploy my Guard, Superhero, and Healer when faced with trauma.

I construct agreements in the place of expectations, committing to following my wants and not shackled by my shoulds.

I deliberately build boundaries so I can forgive myself and others for our misdeeds without being unsafe mentally, emotionally, or physically.

I actively question my thinking, adopting a curiosity stance, to root out cognitive distortions that undermine my clarity and beauty.

I passionately and purposefully drive toward my blissful destiny, letting pain come and go, embracing its lessons with my steadfast strength.

I come from, walk in and toward love, knowing that happiness, peace, and abundance are my birthright.

ABOUT THE AUTHOR

"Look at hopelessness in the face and say, 'we are simply not meant to be together.' Hold courage's hand and walk away." ~ Dodinsky

Dr. Bridget Cooper (aka, Dr. B) is a cage rattler. Change strategist. Thought shifter.

Her ambitious mission is to change the world, one hopeful life at a time. Born onto the welfare system and raised by wolves, she's made her own success, one broken fingernail at a time. Her autobiographical book, **Little Landslides** (2016), tells her story of rising up from childhood trauma and self-harm. Her 2018 TEDx talk, "The Secret to Making Life Hurt Less," was inspired by her life story and its text is contained in this book.

She knows heartache and hopelessness and she also knows the power of the mind and spirit to carry you upward.

Dr. Cooper sculpts the leader in all of us by making us better people first. She does this through coaching, corporate consulting, and leading workshops that guide and inspire people to live more authentic, peaceful, and powerful lives. She's edgy, honest, and cares deeply and passionately about her clients and audiences. She welcomes clients who are invested in transformational leadership and want to step into their full power and potential, who are living life smaller or tougher than they want to or are "winning ugly." She knows her powerful, dynamic approach isn't for everyone and she's totally okay with that. Her mission is to change the world, one life at a time. She works one-on-one with clients to overcome the attitudes, tactics, and patterns that derail their success.

Dr. Cooper has conducted seminars and retreats and delivered keynotes for numerous associations and organizations including: Aetna, United Technologies Research Center, Connecticut Department of Correction, Girl Scouts of Connecticut, Vietnam Veterans of America, Computershare, CCPIO, Gateway Financial Partners, The Phoenix, EMJ Construction, Junior League of Washington, Department of Defense, Allied World Assurance Company, CT Society of Association Executives, Glastonbury Chamber of Commerce, WirelessZone, Connecticut Boards of Education, American Massage Therapists Association (and their CT chapter), CT Apartments Association, Metacon Gun Club, Connecticut Associated Builders & Contractors, Hartford Dental Society, Bethany College, Draeger Medical Systems, The George Washington University, USA Weekend, TANGO, L-3 Communications, American Case Management Association, Greater Hartford Women's Conference, Business Women's Forum, Women in Business Summit, and the UConn Foundation.

Raised in New England, she earned her B.S. with a concentration in human resource management from the University of Massachusetts, her M.A. in marriage and family therapy at the University of Connecticut, and her Ed.D. through the educational leadership program at the George Washington University. Experienced as a volunteer-leader, she served as PTO President for four years, Girl Scout Leader for six years, coordinator for her town's recreation soccer league, and was an active PTO volunteer. She also volunteers for a variety of organizations including Connecticut Children's Medical Center, Junior Achievement, Hole in the Wall Gang Camp, and Dress for Success Hartford. She served on the board of Connecticut chapter of the American Psychological Society's Center for Organizational Excellence and its Healthy Workplace Award process.

Dr. B has five other books aimed at assisting organizations and individuals solve their personal and interpersonal challenges. In each of these books, she brings her groundbreaking ideas and down-to-earth insights and action plans for effective communication, conflict, and mastering change to clients and audiences, facilitating powerful change and transformations in life and work satisfaction.

Her bestselling autobiography, **Little Landslides**, was released in early 2017 and chronicles her painful, yet healing, journey rising up through trauma as well as a guide to readers as to how to do the same. It's been used as a recovery manual for therapists treating trauma survivors.

Power Play, her fourth book and 2016 bestseller, provides a roadmap for reducing the culture killers of stress, drama, and isolation that are draining organizations, communities, and systems of all shapes and sizes.

Her third book, **Stuck U.** (2015), guides readers through her five-step change process at the individual and organizational level, shedding light on the core competencies that make or break change initiatives.

Her first book, **Feed the Need** (2013, reprint 2014), changes the way you think about problems, and strengthens and empowers you to solve them. In this groundbreaking book, you discover how to identify, understand, and feed your core emotional needs so that you can live more harmoniously with yourself and others and resolve any conflict more effectively. She adapted this guide for teenagers in her second book, **Feed the Need: Teen Edition** (2014), with a foreword written by a high school student.

Please contact her to gain her insight and partnership on solving your personal, professional, and organizational challenges at bridget@drbridgetcooper.com.

"I've been attending and running leadership retreats for many years and Bridget is by far the most effective facilitator I've ever experienced." *Board Member, Connecticut Society of Association Executives*

"You changed, and saved, my life." *Coaching Client, Florida*

"With Bridget on my team, I now have a Coach that leads me to be a leader. I had ideas when we began, I now create ideas. I had goals when we began, I now achieve. I had thoughts when we began, I now dream. And what's most awesome: I am led to live my dream." *Executive Coaching Client, Colorado*

"Bridget is one of those people that carries a sense of calm with her no matter the audience she faces. As a person, she is intuitive, a phenomenal listener, and a positive spirit. As a consultant, she is a critical thinker that captures the essence of what is happening in real time in order to translate it in a meaningful way for all participants." *Associate Director, TANGO*

"Oh my God, Bridget, everyone loved you, and I do too! We were so fortunate to have you there. I can't think of a better speaker!" ~ *Coordinator, Conference of Court Public Information Officers*

"Thank you again for all you did for me and us in helping make this conference the BEST one yet!!" *Education Manager, Ohio Bankers League*

"It was a pleasure to work with you. You made my job (conference coordinator) very easy. I've heard wonderful things from everyone who attended your session today." *Executive Director, AFLA*

"Bridget has a unique and distinct knack for very quickly becoming a member of the team she is working with, giving her a great deal of trust and camaraderie with the group. Without fail, she stays focused on result, even if it means changing course during our sessions. Bridget's personality, in my opinion, is another factor that will continue to set her apart." *VP, Information Technology, Draeger Medical Systems*

BOOK CLUB QUESTIONS

How does pain at the individual level translate into pain in a community?

How does pain transfer work across generations?

How do certain cultures become burdened with pain that is transferred from other cultures? What examples can you find in history to demonstrate this dynamic?

How can pain rebelling become a larger movement? How would the world look different if it was the norm (consider economics, education, politics, health services, law enforcement, etc.)?

Where could pain rebelling fit into how we raise and educate children? What would have to change to make that a reality?

What historical (or notable modern) figures could bear the title of "Pain Rebel?" What makes you say that? What can you learn from them?

What historical (or notable modern) figures earned the title of "Pain Collector?" What makes you say that? What can you learn from them about what *not* to do?

When you look around at your family, friends, neighbors, and colleagues, where do they fit (Pain Rebels vs. Pain Collectors)?

What are some quotes that anchor you in the fight for Pain Rebel status?

WORDS OF WISDOM

Readers have always loved the quotes I've included in my manuscripts. I think it's because it's comforting to know that people have struggled similarly across time and space. We are not alone in our slumber, or in our awakening. I included a number throughout this book, but there was a plethora I had parked in a file. I hope these inspire and guide you as they have me.

"The most difficult time in your life may be the border to your promised land." ~ Christine Caine

"Happiness is letting go of what you think your life is supposed to look like and celebrating it for everything that it is." ~ Mandy Hale

"Choose not to be harmed and you won't feel harmed. Don't feel harmed and you haven't been." ~ Marcus Aurelius

"The bad news is time flies. The good news is you're the pilot." ~ Michael Altshuler

"I've found that the changes I feared would ruin me have always become doorways, and on the other side I have found a more courageous and graceful self." ~ Elizabeth Lesser

"Some people will never like you because your spirit irritates their demons." ~ Denzel Washington

"We could never learn to be brave and patient if there were only joy in the world." ~ Helen Keller

"Nothing in the world is good or bad but thinking makes it so." ~ William Shakespeare

Pain Rebel

"Ours is not the task of fixing the entire world at once, but of stretching out to mend the part of the world that is within our reach." ~ Dr. Clarissa Pinkola Estes

"Don't wait for a light to appear at the end of the tunnel, stride down there and light the bloody thing yourself." ~ Sara Henderson

"Happiness always looks small while you hold it in your hands, but let it go, and you learn at once how big and precious it is." ~ Maxim Gorky

"If you are lucky enough to find a way of life you love, you have to find the courage to live it." ~ John Irving

"To play a wrong note is insignificant; to play without passion is inexcusable." ~ Ludwig von Beethoven

"Though we travel the world over to find the beautiful, we must carry it with us or we find it not." ~ Ralph Waldo Emerson

"We meet ourselves time and again in a thousand disguises on the path of life." ~ Carl Jung

"Disgust and resolve are two of the great emotions that lead to change." ~ Jim Rohn

"If you hear the dogs, keep going. If you see the torches in the woods, keep going. If there's shouting after you, keep going. Don't ever stop. Keep going. If you want a taste of freedom, keep going." ~ Harriet Tubman

"Find out who you are and do it on purpose." ~ Dolly Parton

"The most profound personal growth does not happen while reading a book or meditating on a mat. It happens in the throes of conflict – when you are angry, afraid, frustrated. It happens when you are doing the same old thing and you suddenly realize that you have a choice." ~ Virginia Tugaleva

How We Take Our POWER Back

"Getting over a painful experience is much like crossing monkey bars. You have to let go at some point in order to move forward." ~ C. S. Lewis

"Watch carefully, the magic that occurs when you give a person just enough comfort to be themselves." ~ Atticus

"I am interested not in those who judge others after knowing little heartache, but in the ones who have lost their entire sky and still chase after the sun." ~ Erin Van Vuren

"People do not seem to realize that their opinion of the world is also a confession of their character." ~ Ralph Waldo Emerson

"One can choose to go back toward safety or forward toward growth. Growth must be chosen, again and again, fear must be overcome again and again." ~ Abraham Maslow

"I am grateful for my heart giving me three billion chances during my lifetime to start again." ~ Liana Naima

"You can never save someone by letting them destroy you." ~ John Mark Green

"Tell the story of the mountain you climbed. Your words could become a page in someone else's survival guide." ~ Morgan Harper Nichols

"Destroy the part of you that searches for angels in places you know only monsters exist." ~ Erin Van Vuren

"Be there for others, but never leave yourself behind." ~ Dodinsky

"A positive attitude may not solve all of your problems, but it will annoy enough people to make it worth the effort." ~ Herm Albright

"If something burns your soul with purpose and desire, it's your duty to be reduced to ashes by it. Any other form of existence will be yet another dull book in the library of life." ~ Charles Bukowski

Pain Rebel

"The deeper sorrow carves into your being the more joy you can contain." ~ Kahlil Gibran

"It's not what you look at that matters, it's what you see." ~ Henry David Thoreau

"So many of us are starving for life and have no idea, until the end, when we look back and see an uneaten banquet." ~ Atticus

"If you want to awaken all of humanity then awaken all of yourself. If you want to eliminate the suffering in the world, then eliminate all that is dark and negative in yourself. Truly, the greatest gift you have to give is that of your own self transformation." ~ Lao Tzu

"Adversity causes some men to break; others to break records." ~ William A. Ward

"Your life will be transformed when you make peace with your shadow." ~ Debbie Ford

"Angry people want you to see how powerful they are. Loving people want you to see how powerful YOU are." ~ Chief Red Eagle

"Until we have met the monsters in ourselves, we will keep trying to slay them in the outer world. For all darkness in the world stems from darkness in the heart. And it is there we must do our work." ~ Marianne Williamson

"Someone I loved once gave me a box full of darkness. It took me years to understand that this, too, was a gift." ~ Mary Oliver

"There are no obstacles on the path; the obstacles are the path." ~ Zen Proverb

"As far as we can discern, the sole purpose of human existence is to kindle a light in the darkness." ~ Carl Jung

How We Take Our POWER Back

"If you are depressed, you are living in the past.
If you are anxious, you are living in the future.
If you are at peace, you are living in the present." ~ Lao Tzu

"If you are willing to look at another person's behavior toward you as a reflection of the state of their relationship with themselves rather than a statement about your value as a person, then you will, over a period of time, cease to react at all." ~ Yogi Bhajan

"The enemy is fear. We think it is hate, but it is fear." ~ Gandhi

"Character cannot be developed in ease and quiet. Only through experience of trial and suffering can the soul be strengthened, ambition inspired, and success achieved. ~ Helen Keller

"If you could kick the person in the pants responsible for most of your trouble, you wouldn't sit for a month." ~ Theodore Roosevelt

"Never wish them pain. That's not who you are. If they caused you pain inside. Wish them healing. That's what they need." ~ Najwa Zebian

"In the practice of tolerance, one's enemy is the best teacher." ~ Dalai Lama

"Kindness is in our power, even when fondness is not." ~ Samuel Johnson

"Let it hurt. Let it bleed. Let it heal. And let it go." ~ Nikita Gill

"No tree, it is said, can grow to heaven unless its roots reach down to hell." ~ Carl Jung

"The longer we dwell on our misfortunes the greater is their power to harm us." ~ Voltaire

"I'm sorry, please forgive me, thank you, I love you."
~ Ho'oponopono prayer

"Ignoring and running away make us heavy and tense. Forgiving and letting go make us calm and free." ~ Yung Pueblo

"Those who cannot change their minds cannot change anything." ~ George Bernard Shaw

"I alone cannot change the world. But I can cast a stone across the waters to create many ripples." ~ Mother Teresa

"Life is love, Dearest. All else is imagined confusion." ~ Byron Katie

"Forgiveness is unlocking the door to set someone free and realizing you were the prisoner." ~ Max Lucado

"When you can give up your mental and emotional attachments to what has to be, how it has to be, when it has to be, why it has to be, you open the door to the Spirit. When that energy, the energy of life, light, and love enters your world, your life becomes more than you ever dared ask for." ~ Iyanla Vazant

"There are years that ask questions, and years that answer." ~ Zora Neale Hurston

"Do not be daunted by the enormity of the world's grief. Do justly now. Love mercy now. Walk humbly now. You are not obligated to complete the work, but neither are you free to abandon it." ~ The Talmud

"Our own life has to be our message." ~ Thich Nhat Hanh

"I wish I could show you when you are lonely or in darkness the astonishing light of your own being." ~ Hafiz (Sufi saying)

"I thought I was alone who suffered. I went on top of the house, and found every house on fire." ~ Baba Farid

"The only way to deal with an unfree world is to become so absolutely free that your very existence is an act of rebellion." ~ Albert Camus

How We Take Our POWER Back

"Now, every time I witness a strong person, I want to know: What dark did you conquer in your story? Mountains do not rise without earthquakes." ~ Katherine MacKenett

"The trouble is you think you have time." ~ Buddha

"All of our miseries are nothing but attachment." ~ Osho

"Your assumptions are your windows on the world. Scrub them off every once in a while, or the light won't come in." ~ Isaac Asimov

"Have enough courage to trust love one more time and always one more time." ~ Maya Angelou

"He who blames others has a long way to go on his journey. He who blames himself is halfway there. He who blames no one has arrived." ~ Chinese Proverb

"Today is only one day in all the days that will ever be. But what will happen in all the other days that ever come can depend on what you do today." ~ Ernest Hemingway

"Why bother? Because right now there is someone out there with a wound in the exact shape of your words." ~ Sean Thomas Dougherty

"Heaven is this moment. Hell is the burning desire for this moment to be different. It's that simple." ~ Jeff Foster

"Beware the stories you read or tell; subtly, at night, beneath the waters of consciousness, they are altering your world." ~ Ben Okri

"We can only tell the truth when we cease to identify with the part of ourselves, we think we have to protect." ~ Ram Dass

Pain Rebel

"Secret to Making Life Hurt Less"

TEDx Newport, 2018

The draft of this speech, the one I performed on March 10, 2018, formed the basis and inspiration for this book. Please check it out on YouTube and share it with others who might benefit from it. One of my favorite drafts went something like this:

When I was a little girl, my mother invited me to slide my finger through the open flame of a candle. Yeah, some families played Scrabble at the dining room table. My family? We played with fire. Fearful of a burn, my instinct was to graze the tip of the flame. My mother said, "it's not where you touch it that matters, it's how long you leave your finger in the fire."

Painful experiences are a lot like that. The longer you hold yourself there, the deeper the burn.

Our first hurts come early on, often before we understand anything about pain. Sometimes so early that we don't have the words to describe our experience. Like my candle experience, we don't know how a burn works let alone how to handle the flame.

When we want to understand why bad things happened and what those stories mean about us, others, and the world, often trying to make sense of the nonsensical. We build a story around the hurt, a story that has us holding the fire.

If we shove the fire inside, it looks like sadness, self-doubt and recrimination, fear, and depression. Experts call these internalized emotions. If we externalize it, it looks like anger, judgment, hostility, and rage. Behavioral scientists call it "pain-induced aggression."

We are inundated in the news with evidence of pain creating more pain: mass and domestic violence, child abuse, sexual assault, and debilitating mental unwellness.

Putting some stats to these pains, 1 in 4 women experience domestic violence in their lifetime. Every NINE SECONDS a woman in the US is the victim of domestic violence. 1 in 4 girls (1 in 6 boys) will be sexually assaulted. There are 123 suicides per day in the US. 90 people per day die from opioid overdoses. Pain, and our failed attempts to release it, are literally killing us.

It almost killed me, too.

The first time my mother saw my father hit me I was 8…8 weeks old. He felt weak when I cried, powerless to my emotions, my needs. Weak when my mother laughed at him. Weak when he raped us. Yes, us. I was a toddler the first time he violated me. Yet, even after she left him, she'd send me to him alone, for more of the same.

"Do you like it this way?" asked the elderly widower who mounted my 6-year old body, buying my silence with a butterscotch candy.

The neighbor who slide my 7-year old hand through the zipper of his work trousers to coax his "pet turtle" from its shell.

At 15, my father sent a hand-drawn card from jail portraying a half-naked woman with heels and thigh highs pulled up her legs that dangled off the bed. He said it was me, on the phone.

So. Much. Fire.

At 16, I attempted suicide for the third time, landing myself in intensive care. I was defined by the trauma, by the pain.

Consumed by traumatic images, my memories deepened my pain.

And this victim narrative made me a beacon for perpetrators, attracting more pain. I wanted my father, and the men that followed, held accountable. I thought that then I would be able to let the memories go.

Pain Rebel

Pain doesn't help us when we use it like that.

When we hold our pain as evidence of our suffering and use it as protection from future hurts by holding people and experiences away, we remain imprisoned by the pain, and, ironically enough, attract more pain to us.

Like lots of great teachers, pain is so misunderstood. We think it can assess our worth or foretell our future, when what pain is really doing is telling us about a part of ourselves that needs tending to.

Think of the last time your shoulders hurt. Maybe that's right now. What do we do? We might stretch or apply heat or cold. Or use medicine to reduce the inflammation. Going forward, we might commit to stretching more, lifting less, practicing better posture. We might even attempt to reduce the stress in our lives.

We face physical pain on its terms: as information and as teacher about something that needs tending to. If we don't, our shoulders get tighter until we end up with tension headaches, back problems, and misery.

Unlike our tense shoulders, we hold onto our past hurts. Like a coin collection, we inventory, study, and quantify them. But pain isn't meant to be collected. Instead, we can welcome the painful lesson, allow ourselves to grieve the injury, then let that fire float.

When I gave birth to my children I was instructed to RELAX into the pain or I'd make it worse, thanks to a thing called the "fear-tension-pain" dynamic. We fear pain so we tense up, only intensifying it.

So, our approach never brings the relief we want to not feel the pain in the first place, or perhaps to feel protected from future hurts. We want our pain known and comforted, so we hold it to affirm it. To give voice to our trauma. Sadly, in reality, we suffer in an effort NOT to suffer.

NOW, what if we could validate our pain AND release it? And teach our children to do the same?

What if we could find real relief from pain? What if there was no longer pain that resulted in unnecessary pain?

What if we learned that our pain could pass through us like a finger can pass through a flame? That we don't need to hold onto it? That we can focus on our healing instead of our wounding?

What if we could see pain as what it is: Our teacher?

Of course, when we are 8 weeks or years old, we can't possibly embrace this. But as adults, many of us hold ourselves in the flame because we don't pause to consider that there might be another option aside from the burning we've come to know.

Before we remain in the proverbial flame for too long, we can ask ourselves, "What hurts in me that needs healing?" It helps us to see each pain received as an opportunity to HEAL more not to HURT more.

Healing requires us to get out of the fire; to release the anger and sadness we've associated with a painful memory. But how?

Just a decade ago, with divine intervention, my book club introduced me to a book called "The Shack" that answered that question. By using the "f" word in a way I never had before.

OOOOOOH NOT THAT "F" WORD. This one is MUCH, MUCH more profane.

Forgiveness.

Like a lot of you, growing up, forgiveness had always been used against me. When I forgave, I let my abusers back in and you can guess what would happen. They'd abuse me again.

I'm sure I'm not alone in this frightening and repulsive experience of forgiveness.

"The Shack" showed me that I misunderstood forgiveness. That there is immense power for us in forgiveness. Power that comes from choice. In forgiving, we have two choices:

One, when we can reasonably expect that they are safe and won't repeatedly hurt us, we can let go of the pain AND let them come close to us again.

Two, when we can reasonably expect that they are unpredictable or predictably harmful, we can let go of the pain and keep them at some DISTANCE, emotionally and physically. When the person is just too toxic, the distance can mean full exile.

Even if they are family.

And your situation need not be as dire as mine to warrant this. Suppose your parent verbally attacks you and takes no steps to correct their behavior. Suppose your "friend" steals from you? Imagine your boss takes credit for the hard work you do, then fires you?

In all three cases, YOU can decide to see their behavior as indicative of how they see themselves and the world and choose to let go of the pain they sent your way. How close can they get? Maybe you'll remove them from your inner circle. You can opt not to spend much or any time with them. It's YOUR call. You might not have had any control over the painful event, but YOU are in charge of your healing.

Forgiveness means that you get to KEEP your NO by establishing boundaries that are optimal for you and your feelings. Forgiveness isn't about them. Not making them feel good or doing it their way. It's squarely about you and your power over your own life, your personal healing.

When you practice forgiveness with healthy boundaries, you're cutting the ropes that tether you to a past, a past you're powerless to change. But you get to decide your present. You get to design your future.

Forgiveness leaves pain in an unchangeable past, where it belongs.

For me, I got to decide from a lightened and enlightened space how close my parents could get to me; how SAFE they were. That is where my power took shape. After speaking the truth of his debauchery and soul-shaking abuse of me, forcing him to listen to MY pain as I had once FELT his, I cut my father clean out of my world. My mother? She kept acquaintance proximity.

And I slowly, deliberately, clearly, confidently, and painfully released the pain of what occurred in the past AND simultaneously protected myself from undue harm. It wasn't either/or. The two were inextricable.

I kept my NO.

NO to carrying the pain forward. NO to being prisoner to my past. NO to letting those who were damaged and dangerous close enough to leave their pain in and on me.

Forgiveness SUPPORTED my boundaries and my boundaries supported forgiveness.

Forgiveness offered me freedom from holding the burdens of my past so that I could welcome joyful new experiences into my big, beautiful life.

Forgiveness destroyed the power their harm had over me.

Forgiveness was NOT about granting permission or approval. Forgiveness was NOT about minimizing my pain or the damage they caused. Forgiveness WAS about liberating myself from the prison of my past. Forgiving them meant unplugging from the pain, ending the retelling of the story that kept it alive, and, in so doing, finally leaving it in the past where it happened. I took back my power.

Forgiving myself was harder. What did I need to forgive myself for? For carrying the pain forward all of those weeks, months, years. For harming myself in myriad ways with the pain I harbored.

Forgiving others….and myself…was essential in breaking my past's hold on my present and my future.

I'm not alone in embracing this forgiveness journey. I stand on the shoulders of giants like:

Archbishop Desmond Tutu who led South Africa to move on from its painful past.

The Dalai Lama forced from his homeland and sent to live in exile as his followers are persecuted for their faith and support.

Nelson Mandela imprisoned for decades by his political enemies.

The victims of Charles Roberts, a man who killed five girls in an Amish schoolhouse, whose family members peacefully attended his funeral, rallying around his widow with support.

Forgiveness doesn't have to be for a person it can simply be about them, severing the tie you're holding to pain of what they did. Instead of reminding yourself again and again about how you were harmed to validate your experience through those pain stories we repeat, you can step into your power by refusing to allow their harm to do more harm. You already know what it feels like to pass your finger through that flame. You know burns hurt. You don't need to hold your finger in it.

Me? I took my finger out. People have often asked me, "how could you forgive him/her/them?" My response?

How We Take Our POWER Back

"They took my past. They don't get my present and my future."

In Robert Brault's words, "Life becomes easier when you learn to accept the apology you never got."

We will pass through many flames in our lives, because pain is inevitable. But, we don't have to stand in them. When we embrace the power we have to withstand any pain, yet rebel against suffering, we start collecting the light and peace available to us in this short, sweet life.

Forgiveness, the full octane version, often demands that we practice radical, repetitive, forgiveness. The pain may resurface when someone old or new scratches at the wound left behind. We must then return again to lift another layer of pain by forgiving again. People show up in our lives to test our commitment to a life of letting things come and go. Pain exists in the holding on.

For this reason, my forgiveness process is an active and sacred part of my life. Forgiving myself and others daily for their offenses so that pain doesn't set up shop in my tender spirit. So that I don't add to the pain, anger, and rage that pollutes our consciousness and the incessant cycle of abuse we see in the news.

Imagine if we could be collectors of joy and smiles? Love and happiness? Experiences and memories? The surefire way to welcome in more beauty is to forgive and release the sources of our pain and commit to rebelling against the prevailing notions about how to handle and hold pain itself.

One large step in my healing journey was to share publicly my story of rising up through trauma. When life knocks us down, it creates little landslides, taking away our footing and offering up a new landscape on which to begin again. In those transformations, a wise voice calls out across the darkness, beckoning us to allow the pain to teach, not destroy, us. That voice says something like...

Pain Rebel

"You are more than the pain you endure and the pleasure you offer. You are a survivor, a thriver, and an inspirer. You will not be crushed by this. This will define you only as much as you let it. You are powerful. More powerful than anyone who has ever or will ever hurt you. You bear the scars, but you will not be the wound. You choose love over hate. You use your pain to fuel your hunger to know love, to feel peace and share it with others. Over time, you will find people you can trust to heal you, piece by piece. Piece by piece, you'll be whole again."

"You don't have a right to the cards you believe you should have been dealt with. You have an obligation to play the hell out of the one's you're holding."
~ Cheryl Strayed

www.ingramcontent.com/pod-product-compliance
Lightning Source LLC
Chambersburg PA
CBHW021357090426
42742CB00009B/901

* 9 7 8 0 5 7 8 7 1 0 3 9 6 *